LIVING OUT
HIS UNSEEN PLAN
IN REAL TIME

LIVING OUT HIS UNSEEN PLAN IN REAL TIME

A TRUE STORY OF YOUNG LOVE, MARRIAGE, FAITH AND THE UNEXPECTED

MEL LAYNE

XULON PRESS

Xulon Press
2301 Lucien Way #415
Maitland, FL 32751
407.339.4217
www.xulonpress.com

Printed in the United States of America.

Paperback ISBN-13: 978-1-66280-447-2
eBook ISBN-13: 978-1-6628-0448-9

TABLE OF CONTENTS

<u>2 Corinthians 4:16-18 NASB…</u>

"Therefore we do not lose heart, but though our outer man is decaying, yet our inner man is being renewed day by day. For momentary, light affliction is producing for us an eternal weight of glory far beyond comparison, while we look not at the things which are seen, but at the things which are not seen; for the things which are seen are temporal, but the things which are not seen are eternal."

FOREWORD

I AM PASTOR EMERITUS AT GRACE CHAPEL. I WAS CON-
cluding eighteen years with these wonderful people when Mel and his
family were uniting. Charlene (Char), Mel's wife, made an enormous
contribution as Director of Women's Ministry in this congregation.

Because we live in very different times, a person might well stand
in the middle of a sermon and ask the question: *Where in the world Was
God When I Needed Him?* When your wife is slipping away each day,
when a daughter is "living" a vegetive life, what do you do when the
promises of faith collide with the realities of my life? What do you do
when, no matter how many times I ask, pray, or beg for a miracle, and
nothing happens? And most frustrating of all, what do I do when well-
meaning, religious *experts* deliver pat answers, and none of them work?

When we become worn and weary by circumstances, we didn't
expect or see what's coming, when we face events that stretch our ability
even to grasp reality, when it seems we have lost control, we begin to
search for answers and not always in the right places. We begin to read
every book written on the subject of our hurt and need. Lots of well-
meaning people will provide all kinds of trite answers to try to help. But
in the end, we find ourselves stuck on the head of a dilemma: what to
do when God doesn't seem to be there for us?

In the following pages, Mel Layne, with full transparency, shares a
chapter of his journey through life, including prolonged hospitalization
and the eventual death of his wife Char (Charlene). Because of his will-
ingness to do so, he provides us with proof it is possible to walk through

the darkest, most difficult times in life, even if we do so without complete understanding. We may never know precisely why our loved one was taken in the prime of life. We may not know exactly God's mind or what spiritual understanding there is to be known from such loss. And yet, there is a certainty of known truth to which we tenaciously cling.

When insufferable loss comes, we want clarity, and we ask questions without answers. Why would God let this happen? Why me? Why my family? But we get certainty instead, something we can hold on to, something that holds us together. I know with certainty

- Mel's wife, Char, was loved every second of every day by family and friends.
- God was honored and blessed by the kinds of decisions Mel and their sons provided for her.
- Christ's love was evident through the support of Mel's family, neighbors, and the Women's Ministry group she led in her church.
- If every husband cared as much about their wife as Mel cared about Char, we would live in a much better world.
- God filled Char's life with meaning, and her spiritual legacy continues to live in the lives of women she taught and nurtured.
- Char was a modern-day example of the woman of Proverbs 31.
- Her first breath followed Char's last breath here in the arms of Jesus.
- The next time Mel sees Char; they will both be as alive as ever.
- Mel is not alone; God is close because the God Christians worship understands what it means to lose a Godly wife.

In Mel's book, you will not read about miracle drugs and recovery, nor will you read a phenomenal account of divine healing. You will read a story of a husband that made wedding vow promises on that not to be forgotten day in 1960 and kept them for a lifetime. What you will read is the story of a husband and sons who prayed for a miracle and never stopped praying, just because that's what the Bible said to do.

The book is a love story unequaled by few. It transcends life, and now with Char has moved into eternity. The beautiful illustration of three candles in chapter nine captures both the intimacy and oneness of two lovers becoming one. Yes, Mel understands the Scripture reference of "one flesh" when through marriage, two become one without losing their distinct personalities and gifts. This chapter and chapters one and two are worth investing in for your life and marriage.

In chapter *3 to 10,* you will read about the loss of life, but not a loss of love. You will be impressed by Mel's love of Scripture, the love of his four sons, and a loving Christian community that rallied around Char and her family as she transitioned from this life into the presence of God. And you will read how Mel came to understand that oft-quoted and just as-often misunderstood passage written by a man named Paul. This great apostle who knew first-hand betrayal, grief, persecution, and scrapes with death, and who inscribed the answer and the mystery: "We know that in all things God works for good with those who love him, those whom he has called according to his purpose" (Romans 8:28, GNT).

Dan Myers
Former and now Pastor Emeritus of Grace Chapel Lancaster, CA
Author of *Where Was God When I Needed Him? The Question Everyone's Asking*

ACKNOWLEDGEMENTS

This book is dedicated to my beloved wife, Char (Charlene), and her unwavering efforts to overcome life's challenges and become a Woman of God.

To our sons, Christopher, Robert, Douglas, and Jonathan, their faithfulness in their loving Mother. And, in some cases, standing by their father while reaching over the cliff and pulling me back with words of encouragement.

Mom and Dad Layne, as they overcame many of their day's struggles to set a faithful Christian example of living in the moment. Thank You!

Rev. Gene Layne, my brother and lifetime mentor, for his encouragement to continue writing.

Dr. Dan Myers, for without his dedication and encouraging words, this writing would never have been made public. Author of "Where was God When I needed Him, The Question Everyone is Asking" wherewasgod.org

Sue Porges worked with Char in the Women of the Word ministry and became the sweet daughter we never had. Aaron, her husband, and their family, and their love and inclusion of Char and I as adopted Grandparents, we truly loved it.

Our youth sponsors, the Don and Ella Louise Trupp family, mentored us in the faith and witnessed our young love bloom.

David and Patty Jo Yount, missionaries to the Philippines, now retired, that Char first credits as early mentors to her infant faith.

Rev. Dan Jackson and other pastors and mentors in allowing Char the opportunity to dream, grow, and shine in realizing her dream of teaching the women of the valley "How to Study the Bible."

With recognition to those leaders and volunteers of "Women of the Word" (WOW), that are still working diligently to learn, teach, and proclaim the Good News of Jesus. May Jesus Christ be praised as Char is singing your praises.

For all of those unidentified who have served to instruct and mentor us in becoming disciples of the faith throughout the years of our Christian walk, we give you thanks.

Hebrews 13:7 NASB

"Remember those who led you, who spoke the word of God to you; and considering their conduct, imitate their faith."

INTRODUCTION

THE BOOK'S PURPOSE IS TO INTRODUCE YOU TO A COUPLE, Char and I, who grew to love each other in a rather remarkable way from a very young age. It is a chapter in our love story that I hope draws you in and carries you into the exciting, extraordinary, and at times amazing events that we experienced in this chapter of our life.

One person who read the story said it best, "Did you know that most people in this life have never experienced the love that has been spoken of in this writing. Both were indeed blessed and I hope thankful, and as readers, you will be too!"

I've tried to tell our story with the true passion of our love, truth, humor, heartbreak, and hope, with the intent of strengthening your faith in life and learning to trust in God's unseen plan.

While requesting the presence of a sovereign God in the unknown, Char and I tried to remain steadfast in living our life before family, friends, neighbors, and the community.

The journey put forth is one of being mentored while mentoring others, asking all to consider submitting to His unseen plan, that we might be conformed and become more Christ-Like.

Our journey was not one of perfection, but about two imperfect individuals where perfection in all of our actions was something to strive for. It recognizes that it is not our mistakes that define who we are but our intent and desire. He is the only one who knows, to the fullest extent, the successes of His unseen plan.

As you walk with us through this chapter of love and the unexpected, it would be my sincere desire that you will be strengthened to become more Christ-like, even in your successes and failures, as all good and perfect gifts come from Him.

You may be prompted to ask yourself, "Am I really at a point in my faith where I can trust Him enough to let go of my plans, and submit to His?"

Chapter 1

HOPE FOR THE FUTURE
– HIS SONG

SEVERAL YEARS AGO, CHAR AND I HAD THE PRIVILEGE OF attending a gathering of about 11,000 Christians. The program had several leading Christian speakers from across the United States. It was a great time of renewal and encouragement.

While all of the speakers were tremendously gifted in their delivery and presentation, the one I remember was previously unknown to me and, I believe, most who attended. When she came upon the stage, you immediately knew there was something unique about her.

She told her story with an unbecoming voice about how she was born deaf and described herself as somewhat dowdy. But the more she spoke, the more you realized that there was more to her than dowdy looks and impaired speech.

She told how, because of her looks and inability to communicate, she felt the daily sorrow and hurt of being rejected. But, because of her mother's tender compassionate care, she came to know the Babe of Christmas.

In times of despair, she told how she would crawl upon her mom's lap and press her ear to her chest and slowly place her fingers on her mom's neck to feel the vibrations of her singing, Silent Night.

With that, she began to sing Silent Night in a somewhat high monotone voice, with mixed musical notes, some on key and some not. When she finished, you could have heard a pin drop in that auditorium of 11,000, and there were few dry eyes.

Why? What was so powerful about her message that I would remember years later what she said over the other gifted speakers?

Well, I think it was because every one of us, with our own life experiences, became keenly aware of our own vulnerability and lack of control in our life's circumstances.

WHAT CHAR AND I DID NOT KNOW WAS THAT VERY SOON we too would need to crawl upon the lap of a tender, compassionate, and caring God. There, we would press our ear to His chest and slowly place our fingers to His neck to feel His heart and to know and feel the sound of… His Song.

We now sing His Song in a somewhat monotone voice, with mixed notes, some on key, and some not. It's not that the notes weren't clear. It is just that we heard them through ears that were once deaf. And so, even in our forgiven state, we struggle to hear them clearly, and we too sing His Song in a somewhat high monotone voice with mixed musical notes, some on key and some not, as we now hear and see Him through a "mirror dimly… but then face to face."[1]

As we hear His Song, we too will come to know more clearly this "Babe of Christmas" in the "fellowship of His suffering and the power of His resurrection."[2]

In time, we too, will come to sing His Song of hope for the future, accept His forgiveness for the past, and express mercy and compassion for those, who in our opinion, don't deserve it.

The Prayer by Andrea Bocelli and Celine Dion
Only Jesus by Casting Crowns
Rock by The Isaacs

---

[1] NASB First Corinthians 13:12

[2] NASB Philippines 3:10

Chapter 2

FALLING OR GROWING TO LOVE?

CHAR AND I BUMPED INTO EACH OTHER WHILE ROUNDING a corner in the halls of our high school. It was one of those meetings, not of chance, but that would, in time, change our lives' path. After helping to pick up her books, I just felt it was a fine idea to walk her to her class (Thanks for the tip, Mom, be nice). The thing I noticed about her; she was cute.

PIANO LESSONS, ARE YOU CRAZY

Since I couldn't compete in sports during my junior and senior years in high school because of health issues, I decided to take piano lessons from a music teacher in Aurora. On Friday afternoons, I walked from school across highway 40 to wait for the Greyhound bus at Sandy's, a favorite hangout after basketball games. Paying my $.36, I boarded the Greyhound bus and disembarked about 30 miles west, at the JC Penny's Store on Colfax Avenue in Aurora. From there, I walked several blocks north until I crossed Montview Boulevard to take my lesson.

The teacher was more than good with music, but she was a basket case. Bless her soul! She couldn't cope with students who didn't practice or hit the wrong notes, not to drop any names here. I was afraid I was actually going to push her over the edge. If she was in the kitchen getting something to calm herself down, and I hit a few wrong notes, she would know it and shout out, "Play that again." To me, it seemed like heaping coals on her head to request I play it again, knowing I would miss the same notes. And let me say, you can hit a lot of wrong notes trying to play the Bumble Bee Boogie, the 1st several pages of Rhapsody in Blues, or even Holiday for Strings, the easier one.

One time she said, "WE! What WE? We are going to have a recital, and I want you to play Holiday for Strings." Well, I wasn't particularly wild about it, especially one week before the recital when she was wringing her hands and confided in me, saying, "I just don't think you're ready." Well, now there's a confidence builder.

The day came! Oh! Oh! Guess who was there? Yep, you guessed it, that cute little number that I bumped into in the high school hallway. Well, my, my! Now, we are MAKING progress. It is a good thing that I was a gentleman that day, helping to pick up her books and walking her to class. Otherwise, the door for good first impressions might be closed.

When it came my turn to recite, I sat down in front of this thing that I once knew to be a piano, and I couldn't even find middle "C". I knew it was close to the middle of the keyboard, but those white things that were sticking out in the front row now looked like teeth ready to devour me. The black ones looked as if they needed a good cleaning. I think I looked more like dinner to it, and it definitely didn't want to be played.

The teacher, sensing I was having difficulties, HAHAHAHA, had a copy of the music (Hum, plan ahead, lesson learned) and calmly, BAHAHAHA put the music in front of me. I just wished she had included the notes, as it would have been helpful.

After several difficult moments and sensing the other students and their parents were waiting their turn at embarrassment, I took a deep breath, and I played those teeth masterfully, just like I was PREPARED... BAHAHAHA!

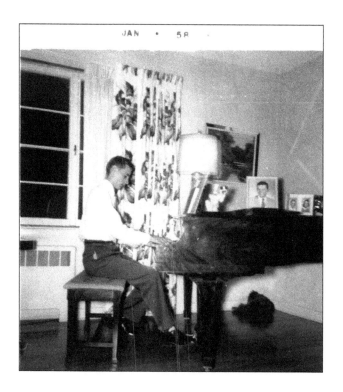

On my way to my seat, I got a smile from well; you know whom. Things were looking up! When I sat down next to my Mom, my hands were like ice cubes. I swore I would never put myself in that position again. But after that smile, I might allow myself to be pushed into launching another possible ice cube hand incident.

A MAN VOLUNTEERED

Char first heard about the story of Jesus when she went to Vacation Bible School. This man had volunteered to go through the community, picking up any child that needed a ride to VBS. That first evening he told his wife, with some excitement in his voice, how he had picked up two of the cutest little girls in front of a tavern in the neighboring town. Each day that week, he took them to the little church 10 miles east. It was there, at the age of six, she heard the name of Jesus. But she did not hear about Him again until this man's son came calling one night when she was 14. She said, "Explained the story of Jesus more fully." Later, she testified that night she became a follower of Christ, not fully understanding how that would change her life.

You see, the man was my father, I was the son, and the other girl was Linda, Char's sister. Lulu's Inn was the tavern (still operating today) and was once owned by Char's dad. He sold it because Char's mother insisted, or she wouldn't marry him.

Char never knew who arranged to have them picked up at the tavern. I think I know because of the timeframe and spiritual awakening that was going on in our community, but I can't say for sure. I met with him a few years ago, at the age of 96, and of course, he couldn't remember for sure either. However, he was instrumental in influencing my older brother Gene into becoming a pastor, and me and my brother Chuck into becoming followers of Christ.

MY FIRST CAR

Between my sophomore and junior years, Mom and Dad decided to sell the dairy cows. I was free from twice a day, seven days a week, commitment to hand milking. Finally, I was free to drive the hand me down blue 1947 Chevy Coupe from my older brothers. Dad said the speedometer registered 47,000 miles, but he thought the real mileage to be 247,000. Hum! Maybe! Now, I had wheels, a part-time radio, no classy rims and tires, and with a rebuilt motor, I was ready. It was certainly not a car for racing, not that I would ever do such a thing, but it did have a heater that kept you just warn enough so as not to freeze to death on a cold Colorado winter's night. I loved that car! It was the car of freedom and a new day for me. But I didn't know how Char would respond to it because she was driving a late model Pontiac Bonneville.

In those days, you could repair a car. But even my dad was worn out from fixing it after 4 boys, and now he took it to the local mechanic for repair.

FRIST DATE??

Later that summer, I asked Charlene for a date. After all, she was 15, almost 16, and I was a much more mature 17-year-old, almost 18, bound for college. While I thought she was cute, for some reason, she didn't like me. Oh, I think there were several reasons, but the one I have chosen to remember is, "I was too old for her." At least that is the one that is kinder to my self-esteem.

Her reluctance in accepting could have been that other guy in her class at school. She was pretty fond of him, and in all fairness, he was taller and better looking than I was. You know, the King and Queen type. Oh wait! They were the King and Queen! AH... Do you suppose he kissed her... isn't that the tradition? WELL, no sense going there now, as the King has long since moved on with a rather fine gal.

The first date was not necessarily your typical date. It was an invitation to meet at church on Sunday night. Anyway, I think her parents were a tad happier with that arrangement too. After all, we were just kids.

I was confident that since I had a Driver's License and the King (I assumed) did not, this might be the time to strike. After all, I was leaving for college in August, and if I was going to make an impression, it probably had better be now, or it might never be.

That summer, she went to Denver to spend a couple of weeks with her Grandma. Later, I found out she had told her Grandma about being asked out on a date by a soon to be college boy. Well, now… Grandma probably agreed with her that this fellow might be too old. There was only two years difference in our age, as I was young for my class, and she was older for her class, so it wasn't obvious.

After spending several evenings at her house, meeting the family, and all that goes with it, there was now a cool sense of friendship between us. I think her parents liked me too and that was a plus! Right? After several calls, I convinced her to go to a movie with me. It was a movie with the handsome and talented Carrie Grant, where he fell in love with the leading lady. It was a "love story." AWW! Perfect! I've always been a sucker for a good romantic movie, even if most aren't like real life. One of my long-time friend's wife and my nephew's wife had observed that I was a romantic, but they thought that Char liked me that way. I hope so, as she didn't have much choice.

Now, I don't want to make too big a deal out of this summer's dating thing because there were only two, church and the love story. I was sure I made an impression, but I was a little concerned about what kind of an impression. Oh, I hate to admit it, but I fell asleep in the Love Story movie. Oh, man!! Hopefully, it was not a light snooze but just a head-bob. Now, don't judge me here, because if you were a farm boy and are not dead tired by Saturday night, you probably haven't been working hard enough.

MEN DON'T WRITE, DO THEY?

Off to college I went, promising that I would write. Now, I didn't know how that would work because most guys read only when needed, let alone write. Stamps were expensive, at $.03. I only called her three or four times that summer, as it cost $.35 for a three-minute telephone call, and I only allowed myself to make one call a week. I don't know that Mom and Dad said I couldn't call more, but it was just something you didn't do.

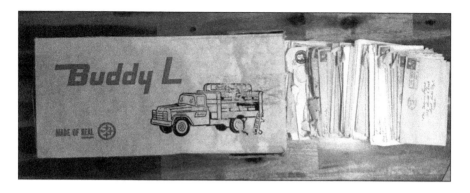

As we both began to write, we came to know each other, and there was a growing feeling of commonality between us.

The box of letters continued to grow. I still have them, and every once in a while, I glance at the box on the top shelf of my closet, being deemed a location safe from the kids and now grandkids. I haven't read them, but I might someday. If I don't, that's fine too. To me, it is more a reminder of what was good.

GROWING TO LOVE EACH OTHER

If you asked me today when I felt something was happening between us, I would say, "I think we started growing to love each other by writing letters."

August 1959

Dear Charlene   My Prayer

          Dear wise and loving God above
Show me the girl that I should love.
May she be good, and kind, and true.
May she have faith and believes in you.
Grant her a smile for each tomorrow.
May she have wisdom in joy and sorrow.
Let her have faults Dear Lord, you see.
I don't want her too much better than me.
May she be steady, firm, and sure.
That the hardships of life she may endure.
But these above all, Dear Lord, I ask,
as I give unto you this task;
First, Dear Lord, she may love you
But then may she find she loves me too.

                              Love,
                              Mel

1922

My dearest Melvin,
          I love you, now, forever, and
always. I want to wish you all the
happiness for I know you really deserve
it. May we always look to the Lord in
everything we do and may we soon find
"His Will" for our lives. I just pray we will
someday soon we will be together for the
rest of our lives.
          God Bless you in everything you
do.

                         With all my Love,
                         forever,
                         Charlene

Writing letters brings into focus a sense of who you are in picture form, something most men understand.

One could say we were becoming comfortable being together and were uncomfortable being apart.

There is a compelling force that pushes thoughts through our fingertips to pen and paper. It is these words that can start the process of growing in thoughts of more than just friendship. It is what I always believed should happen, that growing was better than falling in love, as falling in love may not have the foundation to withstand the unforeseen circumstances of life. Growing to love can bring an oblique picture into focus, offering the hope of a firm foundation in an honest and trusting relationship that would stand the test of time.

WHAT IS CHEMISTRY

For me, the word's "falling in love" seems to imply it was an accident. I think many would agree with that assessment. But for a relationship to be more than friendship, there must be **chemistry** for it to last. I don't know that I want to put into words what chemistry is because it may be somewhat difficult, if not impossible, to define. So, you can use your imagination. But if one is paying close attention, it is most likely pretty easy to spot.

Speaking of standing the test of time, over the last several years, I had the privilege of visiting a man that became 90+ years of age and is now in Heaven. In doing so, I had noticed something that may answer the question of "what is chemistry"? A picture of an 18-year-old had been well-positioned for his viewing from his bedside (There is a story there). When he mentioned her name and looked at the picture, his face, eyes, and emotions just glow with noticeable excitement. Maybe, just maybe... "That is chemistry."

To this day, I can remember the first time I met two women on different occasions. Char in high school, who became my wife, and after her passing, I might have married the other lady that I met for the first time in the church parking lot if she would have asked me. Maybe? I'm just saying… "That is Chemistry."

The next summer Char and I saw each other from time to time. But, I was struggling to find a career path. In the first year of college, I started taking a heavy load of premed science courses, but I lacked the prerequisites to accomplish it with ease. Besides, I've never been the brightest bulb in school. To reach the grade point average (GPA) that I needed to transfer to 2nd-year med-school, there was no time for social life.

Of course, I didn't tell Char because "She was a young thing and could not leave her mother." If she was really interested in me… a little challenge is not necessarily bad, right? She might think I was dating, but I had no time for it. Each weekend, when not on a mission trip, I was buried in homework. With many hours of study, I reached a GPA required to transfer into the University of Colorado premed program. With my last years' successes, the guidance counselor believed I could register for mostly science courses totaling 21 hours of credits. Hello, that should have given me a clue. I was not prepared for that and blew out the 1st semester. All of the afternoon, 3-5 hour labs were a killer for this farm boy. My guess is if someone older and wiser had convinced me that it was temporary, I might have kept trying. But at eighteen, it looked like a mountain too high to climb.

Eventually, I received an Electronic Degree and started working on the short-range Sargent Missile for Sperry Rand Corporation in Salt Lake City. I liked the work, but my partner was a chain smoker, causing me to leave the workplace every day with eyes looking like crying cherries, and I was destined to bleed to death at any moment.

As Char and I were apart again, the letters increased in frequency.

During this time of writing, Char was always free to date. She told me of a couple of dates. But later, when I was able to read her diary, she wrote of a date with a very handsome chap (my words) and stated he was okay, but not even close to the fun she had with Mel [emphases mine) That's me, just in case you forgot. I'm a fun person!

Now, I considered her dating to be a good thing. While life is some-times a smorgasbord, you can't date all the guys, but you can sample a few to confirm you got the best. Right? You know, someone who is fun, humble, and loveable! Okay, so you know the type, not to men-tion any names.

While I was in Salt Lake, my father was injured and needed help on the farm. Being the youngest of 4 boys, I was the only boy that could reasonably return to help him, as the others were already well into their careers. Since it was no longer necessary to write letters, we now began a new phase in our relationship, communicating by talking in person. I liked it!

Most Sundays, you could find us in church as Linda played the organ, and Char played the piano. Our small church frowned on Public Displays of Affection, or more commonly known as PDA. But I worked my way around it! I don't think it was a sin or a secret now, so I can tell you. She would open her hand, and in the palm of her hand where no one could see, <u>I would take my index finger and write the letters I...L...Y... (I Love You). I think it was probably our little secret.</u> Maybe??

<u>SHE WAS CLASSY</u>

It was Christmas Eve, 1959, and because this was to be a special night, I asked dad if I could borrow the 1952 Desoto Hemi V8 that had 318 foot-pounds of torque. It had some notoriety too, of finishing 2nd place after racing the Burnett brother's 88 Oldsmobile off Lady Bird Hill. And no, I wasn't driving!

Earlier in the day, I assembled the proper attire for the evening and shined my shoes, so they looked almost new. I was ready! While trav-eling on the dirt road to her house, I must have checked a dozen times to see if the gift was in its proper place. It was now that the picture of words written in unending letters, once out of focus, was starting to appear. As she got into the car, one of the things I had come to admire about her was that she was classy. She glowed in the winter moonlight, and I was drawn to her like never before.

I turned off highway 40 to pick up Mom and Dad for the Christmas program at church, stopping just before the infamous railroad crossing where our two neighbors almost met their demise. The moon and stars shone brightly upon the newly fallen light snowfall, causing it to appear as a sea of twinkling diamonds. It was there that I asked Char to marry me. It wasn't probably as romantic as she or I had hoped. And the $150 paid for diamond ring was probably not all that impressive. Ok! So, it was not that impressive. But after three years of growing to love each other, it was the right time, even though we were very young.

I said to her:
You are a GEM in the hands of a loving and caring God.
He loves you in every season, every circumstance, and every condition.
Yet his love is not seasonal, circumstantial, or conditional.
He loves you as a friend... yet He is more than a friend.

It is a sad thing not to have a TRUE GEM to care about, to love,
To laugh, to cry, to hold, and live in wild anticipation of being together.
God placed a high value on you, so much so He gave himself for you.
To place a high value on someone is an option, but I have you.
Can I do less... as you are HIS precious GEM!

Love is the "Golden Thread" woven into the tapestry of a great marriage.
By Mel

WEDDING IN THE MAKING

One Sunday, Char and I visited my pastor brother Gene and family when he was preaching in Boulder. The visit's purpose was to announce our engagement and request his services in performing the pending wedding ceremony. While there, a man came up to us and asked how many children we had. Really! We weren't married and looked like it. You know young might give you a clue, and the class ring, rather than a diamond, might have given it away. The next time I saw her, I teased her by asking how many children do you have anyway? Are you holding something back from me? HAHA! Well, at least we added another fun memory to our relationship.

Gene, my preacher brother, has always teased me as looking older than him, even though he is considerably older than me. I mean considerably!! I think people thought I was older because I just acted more refined and mature. You know the type, sophisticated. Lately, we took a trip to Tennessee, and I introduced him as my older brother, a friend of Jesus. Now that is old! Just sharing a little brotherly love.

It was exciting to watch Char and her mother plan the wedding. It is then that the groom to be may feel like an extra. You know the one. The guy that just hangs out off to the side! While they planned the wedding, Char's dad took me aside and, with his dry sense of humor, offered me $3,000 to elope. A lot of money in 1960! But when Char and her mother heard about it, that was the end of that conversation. Later he said, "I should have doubled it." If he would have, we should have taken it. He also offered some other wisdom, saying, "Son, it's not the initial cost. It's the upkeep." He was certainly right on that one, but looking back, it was worth every cent.

We were married at the Galilee Baptist Church in Denver. It was a great day for me, as I was sure about this commitment. Besides, Char and her Mom planned everything, so there was little to be nervous about.

We spent our $100 savings (depleted from flying back and forth from Salt Lake City) on our honeymoon at McLaughlin's Family Lodge in Colorado Springs. (WOW, that $3,000 was looking better). At $8 a night, we had money to eat and even went to the top of Pikes Peak and a few other places of interest. I cannot tell a lie; I kissed her in the Cave of the Winds when they turned the lights out. Let's just let that be our little secret, okay.

NOW THIS MIGHT BE A CHALLENGE

We had moved our stuff and the newly acquired wedding gifts into our 300 square foot $35 per month apartment behind Wanda's beauty shop. It was located about 300 feet north of the Denver to Kansas City Zephyr rail-line.

To tell the truth, I was a bit concerned. Well, that 300 square feet was about the size of her living space in her parent's house. At the time, it was one of the largest houses, if not the largest house in the community, with its spacious 17 rooms. But I never heard her complain once about the rather dramatic downgrading in her living conditions. Guess she really did love me! I know that all of those senior couples in the church adored her.

While I was working for my father, off she went to find a job. And it wasn't long until she found a job as a secretary for the Vice President of United Airlines. WOW, at 18. GEE! Her enthusiasm was damped somewhat when she found out that UAL had some 200 VPs. Anyway, it was a great experience for her.

AND SO IT BEGINS, THIS LIFE OF LOVE, MARRIAGE, FAITH AND THE UNEXPECTED

When Love Takes You In by Stephen Curtis Chapman
The Very Thought of You by Michael Bublé

Perfect Symphony by Ed Sheeran and Andrea Bocelli

CELEBRATING 25 YEARS

Chapter 3

HOW TO MAKE A GOOD MARRIAGE GREAT

WHILE WRITING THIS CHAPTER OF OUR STORY, SOMEONE asked me, "What makes for a good marriage." Well, we didn't have a perfect marriage, but we had a great marriage, and you can too. In this short writing, I will share a few tips that worked for us. I'm not saying they will work for your marriage, as you will need to decide. I'm not a big fan of someone telling you what your marriage should look like while trying to fit your marriage into his or her mold. However, I was always interested in other well-established long-term marriages' wisdom, and I think you should be too.

1 CORINTHIANS 13:5 NASB

"Love is patient, love is kind… does not take into account a wrong suffered."

First, Char and I had observed from other long-term relationships that bookkeeping of past offenses brought little happiness to a relationship. I believe that is true for circumstances outside of marriage too. I was young when I first became involved in church leadership and was amazed at how many elderly saints were hanging on to past offenses from their family or brothers and sisters in Christ. Thus, holding themselves and others in bondage, trapped in dungeons of their own making. It is also true of many in the church today, even though redeemed, still, walk in the flesh[3] disavowing the Scripture to "forgive." The flesh wants what it wants and gives little regard to the damage it causes to relationships. The same can be true in marriage when one or the other chooses to walk in the flesh.

Secondly, I think it helps if you are head over heels, no doubt about it, crazy in love with each other. There must be chemistry too! Love without chemistry is a marriage that will not last. Don't think that I am giving you the impression that love is easy because there will be times, even in some of the best-seasoned marriages, where life circumstances may push love to its very limit.

Thirdly, I think it helps if both are good forgivers. In most marriages, there will be an occasion when discussions about a deep hurt caused by each other will occur. During some of these discussions, Char, in her comical way, would say to me, DON'T TOUCH ME… and we would have fun with that and soon after fall into each other's arms, totally in love and enjoying it!

Over the years, I have noticed that God has granted me a GIFT to deal with the offense, not hold a grudge or want revenge, or an apology, but instead offers forgiveness and the ability to go on with life in hope. I recognize, however, that not all can do this. Sometimes, years later, they are still dealing with it, where most of the time, I can't remember the offense. If I did, it is no longer important to me.

MARK 11: 25-26 NASB

*"Whenever you stand praying, **forgive, if you have anything against anyone**, so your Father who is in heaven will also forgive you your transgressions. [But if you will not*

---

[3] Eph 2:3 …we too all formerly lived in the lusts of the flesh, indulging the desires of the flesh and mind…

forgive, neither will your Father in heaven forgive your transgressions."]

As Christians, we should revere forgiveness, reconciliation, and restoration, as it is not an option but a requirement in the Scriptures. But it is a walk on a fragile foundation because for reconciliation and restoration to be successful, the parties will be required to forgive. The action required in the verse above, "Forgive, if you have anything against anyone," precludes any action by anyone else, but ourselves. This belief must be entrenched in the believer's heart as a matter of practice but may be known only to God. The prerequisite of reconciliation and restoration is a heart that has already forgiven. It expresses the most sincere and genuine form of love and touches the very heart of God. No small feat for most of us.

So, in practice reconciliation remains elusive, and in many cases, unattainable.

My dad was a very distinguished gentleman, partly because he was handsome, with his tall stature, heavy silver hair, and a Godly witness. As was the custom in our small country church, when called on to pray while seated in the congregation, he would stand and with a humble voice, he would touch the very heart of God. It is probably why I still remember this verse and have chosen to practice it throughout my life.

BE ANGRY- BUT NOT OVERNIGHT–NOW READ THE REST OF THE VERSE

In our marriage, from time to time, I would write little notes of love and affirmation to Char and place them strategically so she would find them. Sometimes, I would put the notes in the silverware drawer, in her Bible, or on the mirror, in the shower, on the car steering wheel, or in her unmentionables drawer. Most of the time, she would acknowledge them that day by saying, "I liked your note!"

In days gone by, when someone would hurt me, Char would say, "Why don't you defend yourself? They have no right to do or say that to you!" But sometimes there was nothing to defend, as I was at fault. Other times, my response was that I don't need to because if I live long enough, and they take time to get to really know who I am, they will discern that it is my sincere desire to give up walking in the flesh. A momentary misspoken word or action does not define who I am as a person, other than an imperfect one. Over time, in many respects, I think she became more like me.

There was a time when I felt I had to apologize for an inappropriate, sarcastic remark at work. I meant it in jest, but the tone didn't sound that way. After thinking about it, I apologized to all who were present. It didn't seem like a big deal to them, but it was to me because I saw it as an act of disrespect for those I served. It was accepted, and we went on as friends, fellow-workers, without another word being said. Wouldn't it be nice if all acts of forgiving were that easy?

EPHESIANS 4:26 NASB

"BE ANGRY, AND YET DO NO SIN; do not let the sun go down on your anger, and do not give the devil and opportunity."

One of the reasons that our love survived was because we always tried to practice the above. In practicing this over time, both of us came to the assurance that our love and life together was more important than any circumstance or trial that life could send our way, and tomorrow is a new day with the one you love.

One of the hints that I learned at a marriage retreat was, 'Ask your spouse what you do that offends them.' That can be a dangerous question and should only occur if you are willing to change. After some years of marriage, I found that most of my offenses were little things that I did, and I didn't have a clue that they were offending her. Typical man, maybe. So, communication is vital in this area. Also, listening to her gave me the right to voice what she does that offends me. It worked for us, but each marriage is unique. You'll need to decide.

Sometimes, in marriage, we don't recognize that God is not only working with us as a couple but with each of us as an individual to fulfill his purpose in bringing us to be more Christ-like. I believe when God works with an individual, their mate may play the role of an extra. It is here that the extra has the most difficult part of a marriage, that of knowing when to come back on stage and say their part. There is no written script, only clues offered by the Director. During this time, the extra may be abused and accused. Sometimes justified and sometimes not. They may have tried to come back on stage a few times but said their part too late, too soft, or too loud. In many cases, the extra was not made aware of or not listening to the changes to the script offered by the Writer and Director.

Remember the purpose in Rom 8:28, 29 is to bring both parties to be more Christ-like. To become more Christ-like is a study of Jesus and God's nature, and cannot be addressed herein totality, as it is a book in and of itself. But we can discern that walking in the flesh and wanting what each wants regardless of the hurt it may cause their mate is not Christ-like. The process of giving up our self wants, and to be honest, control can be a battle. There is a lot more to be said about that, but I do not mean that one should become a doormat in the relationship. There needs to be mutual respect and agreement. As Char would say, "Power in the hand of a woman is no more beautiful than power in the hand of a man." Amen!

HOW WE PRACTICED SUBMISSION - EXPLAINED

I know that the Bible says that the wife should submit to her husband in addressing the culture of the first-century Jewish Christians. Still, I think it is greatly misunderstood in many circles of faith today. In many cases, I believe it is taught today with a bias toward a male hierarchy injecting an unneeded bridge of contention between Christian couples and enhances criticism by those outside the Christian faith.

Char and I believed we were bound in marriage together in mutual submission and equality in gender (What follows applied to me also). So, when she came to me and asked a question or receive advice, I would send her away with this goal. Why don't you pray about it, and I will, too. Then get back to me? It instilled within her to accept her responsibility in it and encouraged her to seek out and listen to the voice of the Holy Spirit[12]. In marriage, two listening is better than one.

If someone asked me what was the greatest accomplishment in our marriage and in helping her candle burn brighter, I would say that she had mastered the art of listening to the voice of the Holy Spirit, rather than the voice of a supposedly all-knowing husband. In fact, I think she became much more accomplished at it than I.

There is one caveat. If I thought it would hurt her, I would inform her about my concerns in my efforts to protect her. <u>Something Adam should have thought about with Eve!</u> It offered her the same opportunity to state her concerns for me. In some situations, I should have paid more attention and listened more carefully. But if the decision were about her alone, I would encourage her and support her in it.

The issue with making the man the all-knowing one is that it sets him up for failure. Men have fragile egos, and when they make a bad or a perceived wrong decision, it attacks the core of their very being. In many cases, they will not be able to overcome it without a forgiving and understanding wife. I cannot overemphasize how important the actions of an encouraging wife are to a man in marriage. It is a process that may need to be repeated many times in the duration of a great marriage.

For a woman to reach her full potential, she will need to be encouraged to open her mind to the Scriptures and learn to listen to the Holy Spirit[12] voice independently. It is then that she will have the confidence to lead, speak out in wisdom, and discern His will in her life and family. Husband and wife mutually listening to the Holy Spirit's voice with each willingly in love deferring to the other should also enrich their spiritual growth and enhance their relationship as a couple.

I believe men's greatest need in marriage is to be respected, admired, and loved by his wife, and the wife's greatest need is the same.

EPHESIANS 5:33 NASB

"… and the wife must see to it that she respects her husband."

I do not want to write this as a theological dissertation on marriage. I'm content to leave that discussion to the more learned as it has continued for millennia. Just a word of caution! If the more learned try to understand this and many other Scriptures through Roman laws and culture that I have observed has happened on occasion in the past, rather than first-century Jewish culture, you/they will be unable to reach a defensible conclusion.

So, I will merely call your attention to what we, as a young couple, believed and practiced throughout most of our 47 years of marriage.

We were taught that the first rule of interpretation of Scripture is to understand the text as first readers understood it. Not always an easy feat to accomplish, but I believe essential for correct understanding. This required that we know something about the first-century Jewish culture. I always loved studying about other cultures from a young age, which is probably why I have been interested in Christian Foreign Missions from youth. So, in my study of the first-century Jewish culture, I discovered the following was practiced:

1) Generally, women were not allowed to learn because their role in that culture did not require it as described in Titus 2, and they were considered property, inferior, and cursed. But in 1st Tim 2:11, Paul states that women are to learn in submission, and that was also required of all who wanted to learn. It was considered an act of respecting the teacher.

2) Mostly, women were considered property.[4] And in an arranged Jewish marriage, the desires of young love were not required.

There is more, but for our purposes here, this should suffice.

In Eph 5: 25, 28, 33, God is requiring something new for the Christian Jewish men, that of loving their <u>own</u> wife as Jesus loved the church and gave Himself for it. This was a new paradigm for the Jewish men, and the merging Jewish Christian culture was about to change regarding love in marriage. The word "<u>own</u>" in Eph 5:28 and 1 Tim 3:12 "<u>only one wife</u>" lends credibility to the belief that the Jewish men in that culture had more than <u>one wife</u>.[5] Now, there would be a required change. Generally, young women did not always have a choice in marriage and were pawns to a male hierarchy. Culturally, women were already required to be subject to their husbands. I believed in our early marriage and still do that God did not require women who were bargained for, purchased, and given the status of being thought of as property to agape[6] love their husband. But, if women wanted to live a peaceable life in the Jewish first-century culture, respecting their

---

[4] JewishEncyclopedia.com
The unedited full-text of the 1906 Jewish Encyclopedia
http://www.jewishencyclopedia.com/articles/7954-husband-and-wife

HUSBAND AND WIFE
Matrimony
As a punishment for her initiative in the first sin, the wife is to be subjected to her husband, and he is to rule over her (Gen. iii. 16). <u>The husband is her owner</u> ("ba'al"); <u>and she is regarded as his possession</u> (comp. Ex. xx. 17). This was probably the case in early times.

[5] JewishEncyclopedia.com *The unedited full-text of the 1906 Jewish Encyclopedia* http://www.jewishencyclopedia.com/articles/7954-husband-and-wife The Talmud interprets this as a requirement for a man to provide food and clothing to, and have sex with, each of his wives, even if he only has one.[12]
As a polygamous society, the Israelites did not have any laws which imposed monogamy on men.[35][36]

[6] Dictionary.com 1.The love of God or Christ for humankind. 2.The love of Christians for other persons, corresponding to the love of God for humankind

husband would be an added requirement to the already required submission to him in all things.

It is here that I coined another saying, "God did not come to change
the culture, but he came to change the <u>heart of mankind</u>[7] and in time
that would change the culture." Because when there is a change in the
heart, it will most likely become a lasting change.

I will dip my toe into a bit of theology with caution. If we look
at the meaning of the word LOVE in Eph 5, we see that it is the
highest form of God's love, and in Greek, is expressed as "agape love"[6].
When I read that Jewish women were told to respect their husbands
in Eph 5:33, but no mention of loving their husbands was noted in
the text, I reasoned there must be something else that is not readily
apparent to the casual non-Jewish reader. In my search, I discovered
in Titus 2:5, "Older women to teach what is good, so that they may
encourage the young women to <u>love</u> their husbands" Problem solved,
right? No! Wrong!

Here the Greek word for love is expressed as meaning, "To be affectionate." Now that made sense to me. God did not require women who
were purchased or thought of as cursed and property to agape[6] love
their husbands, but if she wanted to live a peaceable life in that culture,
she would be required to be affectionate; and respect her husband, and
be subject to him in all things.[8]

BUT HOLD ON, AS GOD WAS UP TO SOMETHING
THAT WOULD BRING ABOUT A MAJOR CHANGE IN
CHRISTIAN JEWISH MARRIAGES AND THEIR CULTURE.
(Remember that most of the early church was composed of Jews)

It should be clear to you by now what I meant by saying, "God did
not come to change the culture, but he came to change the heart of
mankind, and in time that would change the culture." Now, God would
have the Christian Jewish men to agape love their own wife, and in

---

[7] Mankind Noun 1) human beings considered collectively; the human. 2)(archaic)
<u>men, as distinct from women.</u>

[8] Eph. 5:22 "Wives, be subject to your own husband, as to the Lord."

time as the <u>heart of men</u>[2] changed, women would become more than property, but equals and agape[6] loved; thus referring us back to Eph 5:21,22, causing ALL, including those bound in marriage to practice mutual submission in deferring to the voice of the Holy Spirit[12] in life and ministry, so that husband, wife, and singles will reach their highest potential as men and women of God, and touches the very heart of God.

GALATIANS 3:28 NASB

"There is neither Jew nor Greek, there is neither slave nor free man, there is neither male or female; for you are all one in Christ."

GENESIS 2: 15,16 NASB

"Then, the Lord God took the man and put him into the Garden of Eden to cultivate it and keep it. The Lord God commanded the man, saying, "From any tree of the garden you may eat freely; <u>but from the tree of the knowledge of good and evil you shall not eat,</u> for in the day that you eat from <u>it you will surely die</u>" (Die here means entering a pathway leading to death).

GENESIS 3:6 NASB

"...she took from its fruit and ate; and she gave also to her husband <u>with her</u> and he ate."

Earlier I spoke of protecting Char, and I thought Adam should have protected Eve. If the man (Adam) loved the woman (Eve) like we are required to agape love our own wife, and since Adam was

---

[9] Eph.5: 25 "Husbands, love your wives, just as Christ also loved the church and gave Himself up for Her."

with her at the tree, why wasn't he RUNNING AROUND LIKE A CRAZY MAN SHOUTING AT THE TOP OF HIS VOICE? STOP! STOP! STOP! IN AND EFFORT TO PROTECT HER? And with one little three-word phrase, "And he ate," God announces to the world that man and woman had disobeyed and had eaten from the tree of the knowledge of good and evil.

Over the years, I have listened to many dissertations on how or why Adam disobeyed concluding, that he loved Eve so much that he didn't want her to suffer the fate of disobedience alone. OH PLEASE... WOULD TO GOD THAT MEN WERE THAT HOLY! THEY'RE NOT!

So, do you want to know what I think? If not, stop reading here and save yourself and skip to the next chapter.

When I read that Adam was with her and did nothing to stop Eve, I asked a simple question. WHY NOT??? I want to think that they, man and woman, were out for their evening stroll, maybe trying to drop a few pounds when they found themselves on a route in the garden going by the tree of the knowledge of good and evil. They walked over to take a glance, and the deceiver struck up a conversation with Eve. Meanwhile, Adam had reclined buck-naked on a non-allergenic leaf while paying little attention to the deceiver, as his mind was distracted or in his nothing box. When Adam saw them talking, he should have gotten his buck-naked self off the non-allergenic leaf and ran like a grizzly bear attacking a fresh hunk of meat, and tackled that naked woman to the ground to rescue her. But no, instead Adam waits and then finally notices that Eve ate of the fruit and she didn't die. Now Adam was worried that Eve is going to be smarter than him! So, when Eve offered him some fruit from the tree, Adam bellies up to the fruit bar like a preschooler saying, "I'll have t-t-t-t-t-two of those S-S-S-S-S-SINSHAKES." By now, Adam had developed a stutter trying to get a word in the conversation with Eve, and Eve wondered why he doesn't listen. You have to ask yourself when Eve didn't die, was Adam expecting her to die when she ate the fruit? Now that is a frightening thought as he stood by and did nothing! And when Eve didn't die, Adam reasoned, "I'm good to go!" God told Adam, in a very authoritative voice, I must say, "The day you eat of the fruit you will die"! So Adam ate, and we are left to reason that maybe this couple was just a little past meaningful marriage counseling?

OK! OK! Let's say I was deceived with too much humor, and maybe we should consider a more careful examination of the Genesis account.

The First Century's Jews call this event "The Curse." But upon careful reading Gen 3, we find that two things were cursed: The "serpent" and the "ground," but men and women were not cursed! As the result of woman's disobedience, 1) women's pain in child-birthing would be greatly increased, 2) her desire would be to her husband, and 3) man would rule over her.

Since women would have increased pain in giving birth, we would need to ask ourselves, should we allow childbirth to happen without doing what we can to alleviate the pain? To me, the answer is obvious. As my dad used to say, "If the man gave birth to the first child, there wouldn't be any more." I agree! But in early Christendom, many early scholars, such as Martin Luther, believed that the pain was women's curse (punishment) and even death was acceptable in childbirth and was her fate in life.

Matthew Henry, a noted non-conformist, late 16th-century early 17th scholar, emasculates women in his writings. If the results of Adam and Eve's disobedience that women's desire will be to her husband and he will rule over you, should we do what we can to help alleviate that from happening? Again, to me, the answer is obvious.

The results of Adam's disobedience and the New Adam, Jesus Christ, can be contrasted. One is holding women down. The other is the example of Jesus giving His life for His Bride, the church. In doing so, He sets the example of how we should be desirous of wanting our bride (wife) walking alongside us where we as a couple grants God one of His greatest desire, that of reigning and ruling with Him as co-heirs.

<u>(1 PETER 3:7) NASB</u>

"You husbands in the same way, live with your wives in an understanding way, a <u>fellow heir</u> of the grace of life so that your prayer will not be hindered."

<u>For the man (and for those women who are farmers or ranchers),</u> <u>"Cursed is the ground and in toil you shall eat of it all the days of your</u> <u>life."</u> Being a farmer for many years, I can testify that for the ground to produce at its maximum potential requires diligence on a consistent basis. For my four sons who are not farmers, and their wives, earning a living requires consistent diligence.

Char and I practiced mutual submission in listening to the Holy Spirit's voice in ministry and life. Couples, in exercising their free will independently of each other, and those whose calling it is to remain single will be required to know, listen to, act on, and be in submission to the voice of the Holy Spirit to enjoy a peaceful marriage or life as a single. Most seasoned Christian marriages practice mutual submission but are constrained from declaring it for fear of being rejected by the church leadership. Besides, the laity lacks the knowledge required to present a scholarly dissertation in defense of their position. Believe me, I understand. As one Pastor stated, "You have to decide on what hill you're willing to die on." That declarative statement expresses the difficulty for those in male church leadership that has been schooled in Christian institutions of higher learning to accept a belief that is not acknowledged by their peers. I respect that! But there are many documented instances in history where leadership, both in Protestant and Catholic theology, were challenged to change, correct, or call out and error. Those who led in that effort were wronged, not by the unbeliever, by the church.

So She Dances by Josh Groban
When God Made You by Newsong – More Life
Listen To Your Heart by Steven Curtis Chapman

Chapter 4

THE UNEXPECTED - 3 TO 10

CHAR FIRST STARTED HAVING PAIN ISSUES IN MARCH before leaving for a short visit with my Mom and other Colorado relatives. The morning we left, she was having pain in her ankles, but there were no visible signs, so we dismissed it and went on our way.

The pain grew worse. So, upon return, I took her to the Emergency Room. They examined her and told her to go home and rest as they thought it was from the trip. After about 10 days of seeing her on the couch, something she had previously done very little of, I again took her to the Emergency Room, where a young intern ordered a blood test. The test revealed a problem in her white blood count, and she was admitted to the hospital. A day or two later, the Doctor ordered a Bone Marrow Biopsy. The test came back inconclusive. Another one was collected with the same results. The Doctor decided she required treatment with a major medical center. So, he made an appointment with a Doctor at UCLA. We arrived there on a Friday afternoon with our oldest son, Chris. The staff ushered us into the examination room and stated the Doctor would be in soon. After waiting for some time, Chris went to see how long it would be and discovered that the Doctor had <u>not</u> been told we were there and left for the weekend. Another untimely delay!

We arrived at the UCLA Medical Center on Monday, but by now, Char was very sick.

When the Doctor came into the room, he examined her and took the biopsy slides from the previous hospitalization to examine, stating he would return in about 20 minutes. He soon returned and informed us he could not read the slides, and he would need to collect another Bone Marrow Biopsy (BMB). WHAT! Of course, I was upset because a BMB is painful, and I didn't want her to experience it again. The Doctor attempted to bring some reason to the conversation, stating this was a highly specialized field. Many pathologists are not trained to place the specimens on the slides correctly. I got it, but...

After reviewing the biopsy, he told us the news. CHARLENE HAS LEUKEMIA! And because she had no immunity at that point, they immediately put masks and gowns on everyone and called for a trained medical team to transfer her across the street for admission into UCLA hospital.

SO WHAT DOES IT MEAN, YOU DON'T HAVE TO DO THIS?

More tests were taken over the next couple of days. Since UCLA is a teaching hospital, different interns were coming in and taking her history. As I listened to their assessment, I realized there was a common voice in "You don't have to do this." And when the 3rd intern made that statement, I asked, "What does that mean?" He said he would send in the Primary Physician, and he would answer our question. In a short time, the Primary entered, and I ask him the same question. He explained that her disease was most often referred to as AML. It's a condition where some white cells have mutated and are no longer capable of providing immunity from disease. The mutated cells are also crowding out the good cells, so they cannot reproduce. Now, the bacteria in her gut had leached into her circulatory system, and if not stopped, it was threatening her very life.

"If all goes as planned, we may be able to put the disease into remission, thus extending her life. But, she is very sick and we need to get her stabilized first, before we can even think about starting that process. As far as the future is concerned, there is no effective long-term treatment. Some survive for one year and a few over 5 years, if they are young. The treatment will be the fight of her life. In the meantime, we will do everything we can, <u>and we are prepared for any eventuality.</u>"

It was then he stated the answer to our question: If she chose <u>not</u> to take the treatment, **SHE HAS 3 to 10 DAYS. WHAT!! 3 to 10 DAYS!** Even though we were coming to accept her condition's reality, we were not prepared for this sudden conclusion.

The Doctor stated that treatment administered to increase the percentage of surviving beyond four years, even though there may be a greater risk of early death from the treatment complications. But it is the best they can offer. Sometimes we are pushed by circumstances in our lives to a point where we would not choose to go. It is during these circumstances that we can choose to grow closer to God or not. That, too, can be a journey and was such a time for Char.

He Will Carry You by Brian Freeze, Assurance
Holding Hands by Steven Curtis Chapman

Chapter 5

CHOOSE LIFE

IN LIFE, WE SOMETIMES GET TO DECIDE, AND OTHER TIMES
a decision is made for us. This time Char chose a chance at life!

DEUTERONOMY 30:19 NASB

> *"...I have set before you life and death... So choose life, in
> order that you live, you and your descendants."*

At 11:34 p.m., April 1998, chemotherapy was started.

The intent was to send chemicals into the bone marrow, which will kill the bad and good cells. Hopefully, the bone marrow will rejuvenate with good cells, with the immune system repaired. Sounds easy. But in fact, it was a passage of unlimited risk in the land of the unknown. It is one of fears within the fears without. To us, it was not a journey of choice, nor one traveled alone, as He had promised to be with her. Now it was time where we would need to crawl upon the lap of a tender, compassionate, and caring God, and there press our ear to His chest and slowly place our fingers to His neck to feel His heart and to know and feel the sound of His Song. God cares, was aware of her struggles, and would never abandon her. Through prayer, we can break the chains of hopelessness, and in doing so, manifest confirmation of our unyielding faith. Prayer is an out-stretched hand, reaching out to a caring God of infinite knowledge and trusting Him, but is not always easily accomplished in real-time.

The passage of life will have in its path heartbreak and adversity, which will cause us to seek a Source of strength beyond our own. Through prayer, we will be ushered into the very throne room of God, who lovingly cares and awaits our entrance. It was there that I found solace in entrusting Char to His care so that she would be comforted and peace reign in her heart during those difficult days that lay ahead.

That summer, 1998, I celebrated 50 years as an imperfect follower of Christ. During this time, I had observed that most of us as Christians study to learn the truth of God's Word, but it's in adversity when circumstances are beyond our control, it becomes alive and real to us. We no longer read His Word as an obligation. Now, we read it because there is no other way to get through the day. What preciously was head knowledge now become a meaningful, caring, and trusting relationship that before was only exhibited in the temporal. For many years we have declared our faith, and again it was a time to live out what we have believed, so that others would seek Him. I'm not saying it will be easy. But in this relationship, we can commit our lives to Him, so peace in the storms of life can be demonstrated in our hearts. And those who observe our peace will be encouraged by our faith, and Christ will be glorified and made known by our actions.

Since the believers are called in the Word the "Bride of Christ," does this not bring back remembrance of the relationship built between Char and I in those early days of young love and getting to know each other? Is it not one of caring, one of joy, one of desiring to communicate through written words, us in our letters of words, and God in His Word? In all of these, we learn to hear each other's voice, and in that trusting relationship, we can fall into His arms and know the heart, and the mind of Him, who we have grown to love and trust.

Some misunderstand this to mean that adversity will not have its sorrow and emotions and that we who follow Christ will all be healed and not suffer from disease or a deteriorating body. And some will even take it to the point that the Christian life will be free from adversity in health as has beset Char. In my opinion, it is an ill-advised theology and will heap coals of guilt and years of sorrow upon those who endure it. Life will not be without its tears and hurt, which will eventually result in our death. Even Jesus in his divine state cried because of others' sorrow by losing someone they loved. But underlying our emotions was a sense of God's hand through this journey of the unknown, and during that time, we prayed for His continued peace so God would be glorified.

Shortly before Char started on chemo, she asked me to read Psalms 91 to her, so I stumbled through the verses. Looking back on it, I'll have to admit that I was reading words, but at that time, my heart and emotions could not and did not grasp the true meaning of what God was saying. But Char did when she chose verse two as her verse to lean on:

PSALMS 91:2 NASB

"I will say of the Lord, "He is my refuge and my fortress; My God, in Him I will trust."

I have often said it doesn't take much of a Christian to live the Christian life when everything is going right in our life. But in times of adversity, sorrow, and disappointment in others and ourselves, our faith is tested, and our emotions are stressed to the limit. This experience was a test of faith and the ever-hopeful truth that He still cares for us.

Shortly after being admitted to UCLA Hospital, Char's temperature spiked, and her blood pressure dropped, placing her in a dangerous state with no immunity to fight the infection. As her condition continued to deteriorate, all I could do was cry out to Him, *"On Him I lean and rely, and in Him I trust."* What was immediately alive to her was now my Source of strength too. I had no way of knowing that there would be a series of crises every three or four hours. Each crisis would have its own set of circumstances, emotions, hurried steps of nurses, EKG technicians, doctors, blood samples, X-rays, etc. Each situation gave new meaning to the words the Doctor said to us earlier, "We are prepared to deal with any eventuality." Somehow in my mind, I thought those words were not meant for her but someone else.

To me, the days were long, and the nights' seemed longer as the struggle for life was held in the balance.

The first night, I decided to stay with her for as many hours as possible and asked the nurses if they had a rollaway I could use. They brought it in, and I tried sleeping on it. It certainly lived up to its name and should have been rolled-away. When morning came, I found myself in a chair, resting my head on the bed. Of course, it was a night of many interruptions, so sleep was intermittent at best. It was then that it became real to me that this would be a difficult journey for me. I needed to remind myself that I was not the one that was sick, from time to time during this journey, but emotionally, I was exhausted!

When the Doctor came in the next morning, I told him about the rollaway and asked him how many they had and how long they had been in the hospital? He said it was built in 1954 and assumed they had been there that long. Jokingly, I asked him if I could buy them all. He chuckled and asked what I was going to do with them. I told him I would sell them to the government, and they could use them at Guantanamo. I was sure the prisoners would talk after a few nights sleeping on them. In the meantime, I had asked our son, Jon, to purchase an air mattress. Little did I know that there would be many nights in the hospital sleeping on it! And since the room was small, I would lean it up against the wall during the day and put it down at night. Sometimes, the nurse would need to step on it if she needed to get on the opposite side of Char's bed.

It took about a week for her to be stabilized so chemo could begin. It was chilling to see the nurses clothed in a protective suit, injecting or hanging the chemicals transfusing them into Char's body. Upon completing their task, they would take them off and dispose of them in a Hazardous Waste Bin. They told me that if they got the chemicals on their skin, it would cause a severe burn. WHAT!

The picture of what Char was facing was becoming clearer still and more disturbing with each passing crisis. Sensing that, I ran down the hallway to the restroom and there, not cried, but sobbed until I was sick, not only in my heart but, physically.

A few nights later, it was an incredibly busy night with one crisis after another, and the poor nurse was running in and out, taking care of Char and a couple of other patients. I was trying to help, but there was little I could do. Early the next morning, I was heading to get a snack from the vending machine when we met at the elevator door, and I thanked her again for taking care of my wife. We were both exhausted, her more than me with 12-hour shifts, and when we got into the elevator that early morning, I opened my arms, and she fell into them as the elevator went quickly from the tenth to the first floor. I never saw her again, but I know God did! And I know she saw a man who loved his wife, and a very sick gal that loved her husband. Maybe, just maybe, God's unseen plan was enough for that day.

Thankfully, the first round of treatment successfully forced the disease into remission, allowing treatment to continue to the next round.

Where There Is Faith by 4Him
I Will Be Here by Steven Curtis Chapman
A Thousand Years By Christina Perri

Chapter 6

THAT'S WHAT FAMILIES DO

THE MOST CHALLENGING TELEPHONE CALL I MADE WAS TO my 88-year-old Mother. You see, my Mother had become especially close to Char. I even think she liked her better than she did me. I know my father did. So, I knew it would not be easy for Mom. I kept hoping that the news would get better, but it was not to be.

For my Mom's support, I asked my nephew Barry, a pastor in Denver, to go to her home on Friday evening, and I would call while he was there. You must understand that I have been very close to my Mother, and it would be difficult to tell her the seriousness of Char's illness. But I knew I had no other choice. My heart ached! I wanted to be strong and tell her without tears and emotions, to comfort her, but it was not to be, nor should it have been as it is not me. I was not very far into the conversation when I broke into an uncontrollable sob. Char, knowing it would be a challenging call for me but unknown to me, had asked our oldest son, Chris, to be with me during the call.

There I was, in a phone booth in the arms of my son with my Mother again being the source of my comfort. This was not the way I had planned. I was supposed to be strong here and comfort my Mom and Chris, but all I could do was weep. I wanted to hold my Mom in my arms and offer her comfort and peace in this difficult moment. After all, I was a grown man, and isn't it about time for me to be her comforter? Hasn't Mom, at the tender age of 88, been too long the one to offer solace and help, again and again?

At first, when I got off the phone, I thought I had let her down, but the more I thought about it, I realized that what happened here is exactly what families would do or should do.

Char was caring for me by arranging to have our son Chris there as a source of strength and comfort for me, and me trying to be as gentle as possible with my Mother, my nephew pastor caring for my Mom, Mom reaching through the phone with her words of love and concern that I might be comforted.

Jon, our youngest, was sick when his Mom first become ill and could not visit but was always around to help his dad. Robert, our 2nd son, lived the furthest away but remained faithful in calling his Dad. Doug, our 3rd son, lived the closest to the hospital, and he and his pregnant wife came over many evenings to take me out to dinner. They were always amused, as I would tell them I wasn't hungry and then eat like a pig once I got to the restaurant. That was because I didn't eat most of the day (my excuse), except for snacks out of the vending machine. I couldn't stay away from Char for an extended period of time, as there was a compelling emotion within drawing me back to her! It was as if two hearts bound together in love could not be separated by time. It is difficult for us to believe that God cares and loves us with the same overpowering emotions. **Now that's family!**

Some years ago, as a son, I remembered going to comfort my Mom a few days after my father passed. I asked her how she was doing? She said, "Last night, after fixing dinner, she went to fetch him." Of course, he wasn't there! When I asked her what she missed most, she said, "She just missed being touched." While I was no substitute for my Dad, the love of her life, touching her and holding her in his arms, after that, I would hold her in my arms until she wanted to let go. I didn't know then that I, too, would miss the touch of the love of my life one day soon. I miss being touched!

Then, I thought that's why we are part of God's family. If we as mere mortals can care for each other, how much more can a loving, caring

God come to us in our hour of pain and tears to gently hold us in His arms. It is also the reason He has given us believers, brothers, and sisters in Christ, for their unwavering faith and prayers, as we believe that a righteous man's prayer can accomplish much. We are to enlist and seek after righteous men to pray on our behalf for healing.

JAMES 5:16 NASB

"Therefore, confess your sins to one another, and pray for one another so that you may be healed. The effective prayer of a righteous man can accomplish much."

The nurse entered the room, chuckling to herself, stating the last time she was Char's nurse, Char had said, "They used to call it blood letting, but now we call it lab work." What a hoot! No wonder Char has needed several transfusions.

Char continued to charm me with her ever-present sense of humor. One that has provided great joy and pleasure to me the many years we had been together. I wish now that I would have written some of her one-liners down. I had mentioned to her that she should have been a joke writer for some famous comedians. Today, I see her sense of humor in our sons. They can be a crack up, especially when they get together and start showing off for each other. Jon says he has my humor. Maybe! He can be a crackup, so maybe he gets his humor from both of us. All four of the boys and their families were a tremendous support for their Mom and were a testimony to the time, effort, concerns, and patience as she once cared for them.

LIVING OUT HIS UNSEEN PLAN IN REAL TIME

All of our life as Christians, we study the Bible, memorize verses, listen to sermons, teach lessons, practice good works, etc. Then one day, sometimes with very short notice, we must live out our Christian Faith in real-time. The question is, can we trust God to come to us in our sorrow, in our time of need? Yes, we can, but it may take time in some cases, and we may not be able to discern it at that moment. Whether in a phone booth in uncontrollable tears or on the 10th floor in a room with unbearable pain, He will come!! And we will not place ourselves in His arms because we planned it, but because there is no other way. It is only then in these life experiences where we learn to trust Him so that we can experience His peace, love, and comfort in a time of our trial and confusion. Look, don't misunderstand. I'm not saying it is easy.

Find Us Faithful by Steve Green
Smell of Smoke by The Martins

Chapter 7

TRUSTING IN HIS UNSEEN PLAN

THE BOOK OF JAMES SAYS IN THE AMPLIFIED VERSION OF the Bible:

> "Consider it wholly joyful, my brethren, whenever you are enveloped in or encounter trials of any sort... **that the trial and proving of your faith bring out endurance and steadfastness and patience...** have full play and do a through work, so that you may be (people) perfectly and fully developed (with no defects), lacking nothing... blessed, happy, to be envied is the man who is patient under trial... for when he has stood the test... he will receive the crown of life which God has promised to those who love him."

Like many of you, I believed that God would punish me when I had done something wrong. Again a misunderstanding of the nature of God! Sometimes we do suffer as a result of foolish decisions. But it is now a great comfort to me in understanding that trials come to strengthen and give endurance, steadfastness, and patience in our faith. We can rest secure knowing the Holy Spirit[12] has sealed us until the day of our redemption.

Some have stated, "I don't understand why God would allow such a person as Char (or any other good person) to go through such a trial?" Certainly, it is one I have pondered over for a time, offering myself instead in her place. However, I believe a better question would be, "Why, in light of man's disobedience when sin entered into the world (Cosmos-Universe) and its resultant effects upon our body with subsequence diseases, aging and death, are we well at all?" In my opinion, it is out of an abundance of God's mercy that we ever have good health.

I believe the real issue we wrestle with is our misbelief that since I am a Christian or a good person, my life should be without adversity and that I will somehow be spared these challenging life events. When you carefully consider what we are saying, all the rest of humanity will suffer, but since I am a child of God or a good person, I will not. Through Scripture and our deductive reasoning, we can determine this is not the truth. To be truthful with ourselves, it distorts what God's Word in totality is saying to us, both in His Word and our known experiences.

1 PETER 4:16 NKJV

"... *But let none of you suffer as a murder, a thief, an evildoer, or as a busybody in other people's matters, Yet if anyone suffers as a Christian, let him not be ashamed, but let him glorify God in this matter.*"

I had to chuckle to myself when again reading the above verse, and I think God did too. To include "busybody in other people's matters" in the same context as murder, a thief, or evildoer, seems to add a whole new meaning to the word busybody. I should pay more attention to that verse in the future.

Holding to such a belief that we Christians will be spared all of life's tragedies denies the written Word. But looks across a town devastated by an earthquake or tornado only to see the houses of Christians or so-called good people, untouched with all others leveled to the ground, to me is preposterous!! It denies that Christians and non-Christians are starving today in the USA, North Africa, South America, Philippines, and worldwide.

It also denies the experiences of the apostle Paul who told us:

2 CORINTHIANS 11: 23 NASB

"Five times I received thirty-nine lashes. Three times I was beaten with a rod, once I was stoned... three times I was shipwrecked, a night and a day I have spent in the deep..."

Well, what is the point then? If we are not protected from life's challenging circumstances, does it make any sense to trust in a God that allows us to suffer like the rest of humanity? If our theology betrays us and says that God is in exhaustive control, why doesn't he stop it?

My conclusion is that this is at least part of the reason we as Christians are here. God wants to make Himself known to humanity. All humanity endures pain, sorrow, adversity, and yes, even cancer, thereby allowing God to make Himself known to others by our response. You see, the real test is not in our suffering but our response to it. Like many in humanity, if we suffer in despair, confusion, doubt, and worry is our faith ineffective and of no value? God forbid! For we know our body is wasting away in its present distress, our hope of an eternal body and home with Christ is secure.[10]

We must never give up hope, as those around us who have no eternal hope will see in us His peace so His Spirit can reach out to them that they may come to know Him, not as a good person, but as Savior, Lord the Messiah.

---

[10] Eph. 1:13, 14 "In Him, you also, after listening to the message of truth, the gospel of salvation – having also believed, you were sealed in Him with the Spirit of promise, who is given as a pledge of our inheritance, with a view to the redemption of God's own possession, to the praise of His glory."

2 COR. 4:14-5:2 NIV

It is written: "because we know that the one who raised the Lord Jesus from the dead will also raise us with Jesus and present us with you in His presence. All this is **FOR YOUR BENEFIT**, *so that the grace that is reaching more and more people may cause thanksgiving to overflow to the glory of God. Therefore, we do not lose heart. Though outwardly we are wasting away, yet inwardly we are being renewed day by day. For our light and momentary troubles are achieving for us an eternal glory that far outweighs them all. So we fix our eyes not on what is seen, but on what is unseen, since what is seen is temporary, but what is unseen is eternal. For we know that if the earthly tent we live in is destroyed, we have a building from God, and eternal house in Heaven, not built by human hands. Meanwhile… we groan, longing to be clothed instead with our heavenly dwelling."*

INSECURITY IN HIS UNSEEN PLAN

I must admit, as Char endured her unplanned distress, I had a fundamental insecurity as to what God was up to. I suspect at one time or another, and you may have the suspicion that what God is up to may not be in your best interest. It is this insecurity that causes us not to trust Him with our life. But does His Word not tell us:

MATT. 6:27,34 NASB

"And who of you by being worried can add a single hour to his life? So do not worry about tomorrow, for tomorrow will care for itself. Each day has enough trouble of its own."

I'm just like you. Even though over the years, I have been forced to lay aside my plan for His, this idea of practicing the Walk of Faith is to this very day not as easy as those who seem to have all the answers would have us believe. Am I correct here? Do you find that trusting and practicing the Faith Walk of the believer to be smooth and easy when everything in your life is up for grabs? Oh, it is easy to live the Faith Life sitting around with a good cup of coffee or lemonade on a Saturday afternoon, when the kids or grandkids are all doing great. You just received a glowing report on your yearly physical, the mortgage is current, the checkbook is not full but comfortable, and you're planning your summer vacation to Europe, Hawaii, Australia, the Philippines or some other exotic place. It makes you want to break out into a good old hallelujah, go to McDonald's for an ice cream cone or release a balloon in the air to celebrate life. Ah, life is good!

But what about the time when your doctor calls to say you had better get to the hospital ASAP, and later he tells you, you had better get things in order, and the bills are stacking up, and the checkbook is empty, and the car is broken down, and the kids haven't called, etc. Let me ask you something? Are you like me and are somewhat suspicious that what God is up to may not be in your best interest? Or am I the only one that struggles with this?

Our insecurity is based upon the false concept that we know better than God regarding what is right for us, or those we love. But His Word declares we only see the temporary, but God sees the eternal purpose. Our focus is on the here and now, and our understanding is limited from His divine eternal plan. This lack of knowledge and experience of God's ways causes us to doubt His intentions concerning us or those we love.

The Book of Romans explains it to us with some clarity:

53

ROMANS 8:28, 29 NASB

"For we know that <u>God causes all things</u> to work together for good for all those that love God, to those who are called according to His purpose."

What is that purpose in verse 29? *"To become conformed to the image of His Son."* Notice the verse does not say that God causes all things bad. It merely states that he will use the bad and good things for His purpose in conforming us to be more Christ-like. Many as believers, stop reading with verse 28. It allows us to believe that all things coming from God are good because we will experience no pain or discomfort in this life.

James 1:17 NKJV

"<u>Every good gift and every perfect gift is from above,</u> and comes down from the Father of lights, with whom there is no variation of shadow of turning."

Sound's fine. But is God speaking in riddles by stating that even the bad is a perfect gift for our good? It seems so! Both bad and good are conforming us to "the image of His Son." So, *"The grace that is reaching more and more people may cause thanksgiving to overflow to the glory of God."*

The conclusion is that God <u>causes all things, good or bad</u>, to work together for our good. Maybe another way to understand it is <u>God doesn't cause all things good or bad</u>. However, the things that happen, good or bad, as allowed by the exercising of our free will or others free will, He uses to conform us to the image of His Son and thereby conforming to, or being in agreement with, "every good and perfect gift is from above."

To be conformed to His image, we will be required to trust God with our life. You see, it is no longer our life, as we (believers) exchanged our life for His. He wants to live His life on this earth through you and me, using the unique talents and gift that He has bestowed on us.

When we became a Christian, we exchanged our life for His. Unfortunately, many in Christendom know little of this truth, even though it is clearly stated by the apostle Paul.

GALATIANS 2:20 NASB

"I have been crucified with Christ; and I no longer live, but Christ lives in me; and the life I now live in the flesh I live by faith in the Son of God, who loved me a gave Himself up for me."

ROMANS 6: 6 NASB

"...knowing this, that our old self was crucified with Him, in order that our body of sin might be done away with, so that we would no longer be slaves to sin, for he who died is freed from sin."

His life is the only Eternal Life. We can now rest as our security is in Him. It is the ultimate call to trust Him with our life where His eternal unseen purpose "to conform us to the image of His Son," may be known only to God but will be manifested in our life by transforming growth in love, grace, peace, and righteousness.

So, is God good? The answer remains, yes! And the pathway of conforming us to His image, that of becoming more Christ-like, is a progressive transformation in real-time, and our life cannot be judged on surviving good or bad, but how we respond to it. It is not our mistakes that define who we are, as God measures who we are by our response, intent, desire, and maybe known only between you and God.

I Want To Be That Man by Brian Free
The Touch Of The Master's Hand by The Booth Brothers
Tell Them That I Love Them by The Martins

Chapter 8

TRUSTING IN HIS UNSEEN PLAN - PART TWO

As a teenager on Sunday afternoon, some of us visited the prisoners at the Adams County Jail in Brighton. It was there I overheard a story about a mother and her daughter. The mother confided that her daughter had been convicted and was close to being sentenced. Sensing her situation's gravity, we offered her compassion and understanding, but it seemed somewhat empty and shallow for the problem at hand.

She told a tragic story about when her daughter was two (2) she had a disease thought to be terminal. And with tears streaming down her face, she challenged God that if He didn't heal her daughter, she would renounce her faith in God and would be His enemy the rest of her life. I believe asking is what God desires and requests, but we trust God to work His unseen plan because there is the hope of peace.

All I can say here, this was not the time for Char and me to question why, because over time, we had grown to trust Him in our Walk of Faith. The concept of trusting in faith is one that in the past we may have put forth in pious public platitudes (The Triple "P" Syndrome), but over time we would be required to live out our faith, that of not trusting in our strength to overcome, but in His power and unseen plan. Only when we are placed in the position where the situation is entirely out of our control, influence, or manipulation that trust truly can be a concept wherein we begin to grasp its significance to living a peaceful life. We can be perceived as really spiritual by our peers in the temporal and speak about trusting Him in faith, while all the time, in the back of our mind, a plan to work it out on our own without prayer or discernment.

But can that be the trust of which God speaking? I doubt it! The Walk of Faith God talks about the complete emptiness of resources to solve the situation we are confronted. In this situation, we will discover if our trust comes from solving our own problems, as humanity is strong in and of itself, or one that comes from knowing and relying upon a Source of strength beyond our own. Many of us can go on for years as every week Sunday Christians or twice a year Christians before we are tested in God's timing so that we may come to know Him as our only Source of hope and strength for a peaceful life. At this point, it is not our place to question why, but to trust in His unseen eternal purpose that may be known only to Him. When all resources are used up, even the unbeliever will look for comfort from a God previously unknown to live a peaceful life.

LUKE 13: 34 JESUS SAID: NKJV

"O Jerusalem, O Jerusalem the one who kills the prophets and stones those who sent to her! How often I wanted to gather your children together, as a hen gathers her brood under her wings, but you were not willing!"

The operative words here are, "you were not willing." Notice He did not say you could not, but instead, "you would not." Our pastor stated that God does not use his Sovereign Power to overcome the human will, as we see in this verse. And in doing so, he gives credence to the fact that humanity can resist the call of God and walk away from his protective benefits. God wants all to come under His wings, but not all are willing.

2 Peter 3:9 NASB

"The Lord is not slow about His promise, as some count slowness, but is patient with you, <u>not wanting any to perish but for all to come to repentance</u>."

Jesus wanted to rescue them on many occasions, and that is true today. There are people in the world today that "will not." Concluding that If God does not respond like they want Him to, say like taking away a terminal illness, they will walk away from the hope and benefits that they have in Christ. In doing so, they set themselves up for defeat and sorrow.

Now, I don't know why he heals some and not others, but I know it to be true. I know He as a Sovereign God can do what He wants, whenever and wherever He wants.

ROMANS 9:14-18 NASB

"What shall we say then? There is no justice with God is there? May it never be! For He says to Moses, "I WILL HAVE MERCY ON WHOM I WILL HAVE MERCY, AND I WILL HAVE COMPASSION ON WHOM I WILL HAVE COMPASSION." So then, it does not depend on the man who wills or the man who runs, but on God who has mercy. For the Scripture says to Pharaoh, "FOR THIS VERY PURPOSE I RAISED YOU UP, TO DEMONSTRATE MY POWER IN YOU, <u>AND THAT MY NAME MIGHT BE PROCLAIMED THROUGHOUT THE WHOLE EARTH</u>." So then He has mercy on whom he desires, and He hardens whom He desires."

During my sophomore year in high school, I had heart trouble that excluded me from sports in my junior and senior years. The problem became evident when we guys were training for cross-country races. At about the 2 miles mark, I suddenly crashed on the course. I didn't really give it much thought, thinking I was probably dehydrated. But Mom took me to the Doctor later that afternoon, and at his recommendation, later a specialist. I won't bore you with the details here. Apparently, it was considered more serious than my Mom and I first thought, as we were shocked six months later when the Doctor said, "You can go back to school now." Mom and I looked at each other kind of like, oops!

The long and short story is that the pain continued to increase over time and took its toll on me physically. Also, Char and I were taking a hit emotionally. If you have ever had a "charley horse" in the calf of your leg, now imagine feeling that pain in your chest on an almost daily recurring basis. But there is no way to rub it to get relief.

Later, when we told our church family that more tests would be scheduled, the women decided to have a group prayer day for me, and I'm sure others'. Now, as a young man with a wife and family of 3 boys at the time, they were genuinely concerned for us. I think because of their prayers, God healed me. Healing was <u>not</u> something talked about very much in our circle of faith, so little was made of it.

As a young kid, I always seemed to get everything first (mumps, measles, chickenpox, pneumonia, polio, etc.). I think it was so I could have everything twice. Ok, maybe not! I'm not that special.

For Char, while I wanted her healed and with me for life, I choose to trust Him. With what I had experienced in life, you would have thought that Char's struggle for life would have been easier for me. Right?

MARK 14:33-37 NASB

"And He (Jesus, emphasis mine) took with Him Peter and James and John, and began to be very distressed and troubled. And He said to them, <u>"My soul is deeply grieved to the</u>

point of death; remain here and keep watch." He then went a little beyond them, and fell to the ground and began to pray that if it were possible, the hour might pass by. And he was saying, "Abba! Father! All things are possible for you; remove this cup[11] from Me; yet not what I will but what You will." And He came and found them sleeping."

CHARLES SPURGEON

"If the royal divine Son of God was not exempt from the rule of asking, you and I cannot expect the rule to be relaxed for us."

Are we indeed at a point in our faith life, when partitioning to Him in prayer, where we can trust Him enough to let go of our plans and life and submit to His unseen plan? Now, all things are possible with God, but God is not obligated to perform according to our wishes or desires because we cannot understand or see His unseen plan, and He can show mercy to whom he wants. In our prayers, let us be more concerned about God being made known to many and glorified in what is present or to come in our life. Is this not what Jesus wanted when he spoke about Lazarus?

JOHN 11:3-4 NASB

... "so the sisters sent word to Him, saying, "Lord, behold, he who you love is sick. But when Jesus heard this, He said, "This sickness is not to end in death, but for the glory of God, so that the Son of God may be glorified by it."

---

[11] Jesus willing took on the sins of the world, and they crushed him.

John 3:16 For God so loved the world, that He gave His only Son, that whosoever believes in him shall not perish, but have Eternal life.

1 John 5:11-12 And the testimony is this, that God has given us eternal life, and this life is in His Son. He who has the Son has the life; He who does not have the Son of God does not have life.

As I prayed for my wife to be healed, I wanted God to be glorified and honored through whatever conditions were to come.

JOHN 11: 7, 14, 15, 25, NASB

"He said to his disciples, V.7, "Let us go to Judea." V.14, 15 Jesus said to them plainly, Lazarus is dead, and I am glad for your sakes that I was not there, <u>so that you may believe.</u> V.25 Jesus said to her, I am the resurrection and the life; <u>he who believes in Me will live even if he dies, and everyone who lives and believes in me will never die, do you believe this.</u>" She said to Him, Yes, Lord; I believe that you are the Christ, the Son of God, even He who comes into the world."

JOHN 12 10-11 NKJV

"Now a great many of the Jews knew that He was there; and they came, not for Jesus' sake only, but that they might also see Lazarus, whom He had raised from the dead. But the chief priests plotted to put Lazarus to death also, because on account of him many of the Jews went away and believed in Jesus."

Jesus called Lazarus out of the grave after being dead for four days and told them to take off the binding and release him. Later, <u>Jesus rose from the grave and was seen by hundreds.</u> Why didn't the Jewish leaders believe it? I think it was because they feared losing control and their esteemed position in Judaism.

Lazarus escaped the wrath of the Jewish leaders by going to the Island of Cyprus. In 890AD, Lazarus' coffin was discovered and was inscribed with these words: **Lazarus, four days dead, friend of Christ.**

There is archeological and historical proof that Lazarus died the second time on the Island.

Jesus, as God-man, felt the sorrow and loss in His future destiny. He also felt the sadness of Lazarus' sisters as they endured his loss. These very emotions, given by God, cause us to pray for each other out of genuine love and concern. It directs us to reach past the feelings of loss and sorrow. If we are to grow in our Walk of Faith, all of us will someday pass through a time of trials and testing where the outcome is entirely out of our control. It will be a time of learning to trust Him, as now not a source but The Source of our strength, and we willingly submit to His unseen plan while continuing to pray that He will be <u>glorified, and many will come to know Him through it</u>. The result will be moving away from the Walk of Faith and trust in Him, as the woman whose daughter was in prison, or it will be a time of coming to trust, hope, peace, and caring for others, even if they can't care for us <u>as the disciples also fell asleep</u>. How about you? How about me?

<u>KNOWN ONLY TO ME</u>

Ongoing crises and the lack of sleep can play tricks on your mind and cause you to seek solace outside of the present, as the mind wants to escape reality. So, while Char was sleeping, I continued working on several projects that needed completion for my work. It was a good distraction but added even more pressure to a body wanting to surrender.

I felt inept at giving Char the care she needed when she was home. You see, Home Care, in my mind, was providing support with someone who does that kind of thing professionally. But Home Care, in this case, was me being the professional. It was I hanging the bags of meds on the tree, giving the shots, injecting a saline solution into her mainline to keep it open, while hoping beyond hope that the effort would bring healing.

A lady across the hall had the same illness as Char and past. The young man next-door, with a treatable brain tumor, accidentally overdosed and now paralyzed. After eighteen months of treatment and several experimental drugs, the skin and bone lady observed in the hallway was now without hope of recovery. Only I knew all of the above.

Char had decided on an experimental drug to see if it might help her treatment, and if not her, maybe someone. The experimental drug was in powder form and had to be mixed with a solution for injection. The amount required was small and given with a small vial and needle. You had to swirl, not shake it when mixing. After consulting with the nurse on her home visit, the first night, and after she consulted with the Doctor on the correct dosage, it was now my job to mix it and give Char the injection. With the knowledge of the above embedded in my mind, it took over an hour to build up the courage to give her the first injection.

The insecurities and the lack of confidence for a man who typically could rise to the occasion were heart-wrenching for me but only known to me. Truthfully, no caregiver is just fine, particularly when caring for someone they love with a terminal illness. They are fine because, through the trials of life, they are growing in their Walk of Faith, giving them strength where they are compelled to endure out of an abundance of LOVE. We vowed in our marriage to love and cherish in sickness and in health. It seemed like such a small thing at the time. But, in real life, it can be daunting and a life-altering process. It may be the most rewarding and yet challenging event that came into our marriage but has had a long-lasting influence upon my acceptance of love, life, and relationships for the future.

The Bible says love never fails. I believe that in the sense that God's love is eternal and lasting! Love can be expressed in giving of oneself, as Christ gave his life for the believer. Sometimes, in a marriage, love becomes not the passion that is so often expressed openly by young love but maybe observed only by others as a life commitment.

<u>THE GIFT OF LASTING LOVE</u>

During this time, the rest at home allowed us to celebrate our 38th wedding anniversary. We usually would tell everyone we've had 35 years of marital bliss. Those who have been married for some time know what we speak, but some newlyweds may need help figuring out the meaning. Ha! Nevertheless, it was a great time of remembering the "Gift of Love" that God had given us. It is a gift that many in life have not had the joy of experiencing and knowing that we were truly thankful.

You Say by Lauren Daigle
Together by Steven Curtis Chapman
Some Times It Takes A Mountain by The Gaither Vocal Band

Blow Her Candle Out? Really!

In recent years, I have noticed something unique in the wedding ceremony. I like it and understand that it represents "oneness."

On a table off to the side are three candles. The one on the left represents the Bride, and the one right represents the Groom, and each is glowing brightly during the ceremony. At some point when the preacher has either lost his place in his wedding book or ran out of things to say, the Bride and Groom move in front of the table, and each takes their candle and lights the middle candle indicating they are "one." It is very touching, and I have seen some tears shed during this time. There was a time or two when I felt a teardrop in my eyes.

One thing that has always been very interesting to me is what happens next. The Bride and Groom blow out their candles. Now, I have to admit if Char knew her candle would get blown out in marriage, she might not have accepted my marriage proposal. If I had thought more about blowing out my candle, I might have elected to miss the ceremony.

Many of you who have done this at your wedding, don't be upset at me. Truly, I do understand its meaning!! However, after some years of experience in marital bliss, I can say with some certainty:

I believe the purpose of a great marriage is for each to give to the other in such a way that their candle burns brighter.

Over past years, and sometime in the future, each of us independently of the other will go through an experience where our candle will flicker beneath the winds of change. It seems that marriage works best when we look at what our mate is struggling with and do everything we can to ensure their candle doesn't flicker and blow out, BUT BECOMES BRIGHTER. For me, it was a learning experience to try and help Char reach her full potential as an individual, as a Woman of God, and that her candle would burn brighter.

Shortly after our honeymoon, I came home from harvesting and found her reading a Children's Bible. At first, I thought, oh man, she wants to have kids, this soon!! Char said that every time we found out that we were having another child, I started another business or found an additional job. There is nothing like getting an early start since a child brings with it a lifetime commitment. I would tease her that I would hold them only after they were potty trained or three years old. But when I saw our first son, Chris, I couldn't wait to get my hands on him in that room with all the babies. He and the boys to come, Robert, Douglas, and Jonathan were part of us forever; that is a family.

After some conversation, I realized she was trying to understand the Bible, as it was a significant part of my life.

Because I was sick so much as a kid, Mom had enrolled me at some point in a Navigator's Bible memorization plan. It required some discipline, and I had little of that, but I was proud of the new Bible that my parents had purchased for me. It was later that Mom said, "I had memorized some 350 verses." Well, maybe, but if she would have asked me to quote them to her the next week, or even that day, I probably could not cite them accurately, if at all. I didn't know then that the effort would be a source of blessing to me in the years ahead as God brought some to remembrance on many occasions.

So, when Char took an interest and started asking me questions about the Bible, she would say, "How did you know that?" It was then that I determined in my heart that I needed to do everything possible for her to learn and reach her full potential as a Woman of God, as it was her desire too. Thankfully, many others saw that desire in her life, and all worked toward a common goal. I don't know how she would view it, but later in life, instead of her asking me questions, I was asking her questions. When we were through discussing a theological question, she would say with her usual humor, "We are now confused on a higher level." But it was fun and nonthreatening to both. I miss it!

Char's interest in learning more about her faith was interrupted to some degree by being a Mom. Together with a strong desire to learn more about her faith, her tenacity could seldom be matched. Over many years, she became a knowledgeable and gifted Bible scholar. At last count, she had deeply studied over 34 books of the Bible and had extensive knowledge of the complete Bible. Her training, desire, sheer dedication to daily study guided her in becoming a gifted and cherished Woman of Faith. As her husband, may I say, "She was always classy!"

THE FINAL ROUND OF TREATMENT

This round of treatment for Char is an "all or nothing."

Before approving the procedure, they informed us that the chance of killing all the cancerous cells was slim to none, but it was the best they could offer. Now, they would use Radiation together with Chemotherapy in hopes of killing the remaining cancerous cells. It is during this time she will need more transfusions. It would be a daunting and unnerving experience.

Once that is accomplished, the stem cells that had been previously harvested and held in suspension by freezing would be ready for transplant. The overall procedure is a dangerous process and is potentially life-threatening, carrying with it uncertain risks. Still, it is the only option available that offers a long-term solution, meaning more than a year. During this time, her candle would flicker and struggle to keep from being extinguished by the winds of change. I was there to offer whatever I could. It was a continuing time to trust, as she was in the hands of medical professionals and a caring and compassionate God. At this point, her Walk of Faith will be challenged, and her candle will flicker. It is a lesson that we all learn in marriage, sooner or later, that I could not meet all of Char's needs, nor can she meet all my needs, nor was that what God intended in marriage. I believe it was intended that after we surrender to Christ to meet our needs, by our submission to Him, then and only then can our needs be met by our spouse. It is a process requiring a lifetime of effort.

Sometimes a man cannot discern what is needed to make their mate happy, even though she may have pointed it out on several occasions! In Char's present distress, I could offer her a look across the room that says I love you and have an understanding heart that can be felt without speaking a word. I can read to her when she can no longer read, as the drugs blurred her vision. I can, in her darkest hour, slip into the chapel on the first floor in the wee hours of the night and offer a bleeding heart before the throne of God. Not a heart that demands God's healing, but one that entrusts her to the Sovereign will of a God who loves her as only He can.

By trusting Him, I can assure myself that I am doing the most to see her CANDLE BURNS BRIGHTER.

THE EXTRA

Our youngest son, Jonathan (Jon), was in elementary school when his mother worked with him to memorize a small part in the class Christmas play. Jon has a quick mind, and he had memorized the Christmas story in Luke chapter 2. Mom would stand him on a chair, and he would practice saying his part. It took Mom a while to help him know when to come in a say his part loud enough so everyone could hear him, but not too loud that it would embarrass his parents. Finally, the big day came, and many other parents, minus some fathers and mothers who couldn't get off work, crowded into the classroom in wild anticipation and some fear of embarrassment. I remember seeing Jon off to the side, totally oblivious to his father's anxiousness biting his lip nervously.

Soon, the program began. When it was Jon's turn to speak, he stood tall and said his part at the right time, not too loud as to embarrass his parents, but just loud enough, so the people in the back row heard his words above the heating unit, and the pounding heart and rapid breathing of his father. Yep, Jon was there. He said his part at the right time, not too soon, not too late, not too loud, and not too soft. You might say that Jon's role was a "bit part," or as Hollywood calls them, an "extra." I don't know that I like being referred to as an extra. To me, it just seems to refer to someone who just happened to walk by the stage at a given time and was taken advantage of as not being needed, but the play seemed better with him there.

I have never been much more than a bit player or an extra in the greater stage of this life. During this round of Chemo, Char had the leading role. The doctors were the directors, and the nurses got the credits, as they did all the work. But off to the side was me, the extra. I was somewhat biting my lip in uneasiness, praying that when I stumble on to the stage that I would know when to come in, I would say my part at the right time, not too loud to embarrass myself, not too soft so that Char couldn't hear it. It has been indeed my greatest desire to hear someday the words of my Lord say to me, "You knew when to come in, and you said your part not to loud, and not to soft, that her candle might burn brighter. Well done my son."

Let me ask you, are you doing something to help someone's candle burn brighter while they endure a difficult struggle? It is the greatest challenge, and to experience life to its fullest, you must give it your full attention.

The   Promise   by   The   Martins

When I Said I Do by Clint Black

10,000 Reasons – Bless The Lord Oh My Soul by Matt Redman

Chapter 10

A WORD STUDY CUTE OR ACUTE

THERE ARE THOSE IN THE CHRISTIAN FAITH WHO BELIEVE that we should have trusted God for healing, and if our faith were strong enough, Char would have been healed. I would not presume to make that decision for you. But let me suggest if you had to choose at age 56 and were told you had 3 to 10 days to live, what choice would you make? Then, that is your answer.

A BRIEF INTERLUDE BEFORE THE FINAL CHEMO

On Sunday, the kids and grandkids came home to visit Char before entering the hospital for her final treatment. They are so cute! Robert had arrived midday with his family, as he lived the furthest away. So, his infrequent meetings with his Mom were always exceptional, as they had a special relationship. While he can display the impression as being a rough and tough businessman on the outside, on the inside, he is a kind, gentle, understanding, and compassionate son. It not only makes his Dad proud, but he shows those emotions best when he is with his Mom. That day was not a relaxed one for him, as seeing his Mom in this state of a weakening body was difficult and challenging. But, despite it, he encouraged and gave hope to a Mom in need of his love.

Robert always seemed to perform at a level that the rest of us could only hope to achieve. So, when I heard them laughing, I remembered his accomplishments on his 16th birthday. He got his driver's license, his pilot's license, and 25 demerits at school. Also, he took his Mom for her first small plane ride, on a particularly windy afternoon. Trust me! I'm not sure she would have done that for the rest of us guys.

Now the word "CUTE" congers up all kinds of descriptive adjectives, such as adorable, sweet, and cuddly. Certainly, the grandkids were all of that, and we had a great time.

LEARNING NEW WORDS.

In addition to learning several new medical terms these months, I have realized that the addition of one seemingly insufficient letter to a word can change the meaning dramatically. Take the word "cute." I like the word. It brings to mind the first time I noticed Char. Grandkids are cute! Char is cute! It would seem to me, and I would like to think that the medical "wordologist" (to coin a new word) could come up with a word not so close to cute to describe a disease like "Acute Myeloid Leukemia." How dare they dramatically change a word's, meaning by adding one little, seemingly insignificant letter ("A").

I don't like the word "Acute" near as good as the word "Cute." After all, some new interns learning medical words like I am might come out of the delivery room and say, "you have an acute baby." It seems that it should take more than one letter to change the meaning of a word so dramatically. Oh, I am sure the people in the hallowed halls of higher education are not concerned about my word study. After all, I am an extra. But if you happen to play the leading role, maybe you could form a society to change some medical words. You could be the President. Maybe we could find nurses to do the work. I'll stand off to the side, as I'm an extra.

I had some tests completed on my heart at one point in my life. The report came back that they were rather "unremarkable." To me, that means bad. But not in the medical world where it means GOOD, at least in this case! Hum! Confusing!

Okay, so maybe I carried it a little too far. But isn't it great to know when we are called to Heaven that God will not change the word "grace" to "race"? After all, He could change the word if anybody could. He could say, "I am sorry, but you didn't finish the race on time; the race was on Tuesday, not Wednesday or you started too fast and you are disqualified so, I'm not going to let you into Heaven because I have changed grace to race. It is obvious you can't follow the rules of the race."

Now, don't get me wrong, rules are good, sometimes. The only reason I didn't run away from home when I was five is that Mom wouldn't let me cross the street, actually a country dirt road. So, I went to the front yard and sat under a tree with a lunch that Mom had packed. But, I was glad when suppertime came. Since my ability to remember why I was on the front lawn was no longer important, I was happy to hear Mom call, "It's time to eat."

That night when Mom put me in bed and gave me a big hug, I was thankful for the rule: "Don't cross the street." Just like Mom, God has rules to protect us. Sometimes, we break some of those rules in the race of life, but I will always be Mom and Dad's son and God's son. That is the reason I like the word "grace" better than the word "race." God isn't going to change the word grace by dropping one little seemingly insignificant letter to make it a competitive "race." Oh, I know the apostle Paul told us to run the race set before us and follow the rules to receive the prize. But there would be no PRIZE, RULES, OR RACE WITHOUT GOD'S FORGIVING GRACE.

His Enabling Grace gives us the resources to endure life's trials while building our endurance to continue the race of life. That is the reason I like the word grace. It enables us to go through trials because we know our position is secure in Him. I want to encourage you to rest in His Word because His Spirit seals us until the day of our redemption. Receive courage and hope!

Why Can't We by The Isaac
I Love You More by The Isaacs
I Still Trust You by The Isaacs

Chapter 11

4ᵀᴴ FLOOR YOU GOTTA BE KIDDING ME!

TAKE TIME TO LEARN HIS WORD BECAUSE CHAR FOUND most of her peace in past Scripture's learned. They are hard to learn when the morphine and pain cloud your mind making it difficult to concentrate. As she said, it "Makes her goofy," but allows her to think for a moment that everything is okay. This is not the time to learn new truths from His Word, but to rest in lessons already learned.

After almost 24 weeks of sitting and walking the hospital halls, I decided I needed more exercise. Really, it was kind of out of character for me because I'm not that smart. Usually, when I had thought of needing more exercise, I would take a nap until the feeling passed.

So, I started up the stairs to the tenth floor only to lose it at the door marked "four" (I think there is a country song there, don't you). I assume to this day that it was marked wrong. I was not out of air, but my chicken legs could no longer carry me, so I was off to find the elevator! I had been thinking earlier that if I could give Char some of my strength, then maybe, just maybe, she could feel a moment of wellness. How foolish of me to think such a thing because I am weak in the flesh, and the only thing that could carry her is God's mercy and grace. I like the words "cute" and "grace" better than the words "acute" and "race," because sometimes in the race of life, we don't have the strength and must rely totally upon His enabling grace. I like the word grace!

When asleep, her body jerked and twitched as the struggle for wellness raged. During this time of waiting, one can feel alone, deserted, and afraid... including her soul mate. The book of Hebrews says:

HEBREWS 13:5 KJV

"...for He hath said, I will never leave thee, or forsake thee."

I like the word "never." He could have said, "I'll never forget you provided you make all of the right decisions in life" or, "Good only if you return proof of Baptism within ten days of the event." I like the words "cute," "saving grace," "enabling grace," and "never." Even though Char's head had become as bald as a peeled onion, I still thought she was cute. He will never disown or abandon her! He will never disown or abandon me! He will never disown or abandon you IN CHRIST.

Our insecurity can drive our minds to believe that God had abandoned her. Those days of questioning is when doubt and fear grip our emotions and cause us to wonder if what God is doing is in her best interest. Over that last 6-7 months, Char had required constant medical treatment requiring 31 red blood cell transfusions and 19 platelet transfusions. 15 days in Antelope Valley Hospital. 87 days at UCLA Medical Center, with brief periods in housing across the street from the hospital or at home. The statistics make all that had happened during this event in her life to seem rather matter of fact. Instead, it was a challenging journey, requiring the gentle touch and consoling heart from a caring God for her and the family.

During her last treatment in the hospital, Char was again on the 10th floor, and I was 5 days on the 5th floor, with a kidney stone. Most of you, like me, have at one time in your life asked God the question, "What was the real purpose here?" Can any good come out of me having a kidney stone, particularly right when I was needed? Could it be that it was for me? Maybe I could learn something from this time of pain. Was it so I could trust God to take care of Char when I'm not there? Was it so Char could trust God to take care of her when we are apart? Was it just one of those events in life that happens and really, as far as we can see, served no eternal purpose? But could it have been part of His unseen plan and known only to Him?

SECOND GRADER - WHAT!!

In the 5th grade, I remember when all of the boys from the 5th to the grade 8th were instructed to go downstairs to the 2nd-grade room. Upon arriving, we were positioned to stand at the front of the class. No one knew what was going on except we were all delighted to get out of class unexpectedly. At least some things never change. I didn't know until later that morning that I had been selected, out of all the boys, of having the dubious distinction as being the scoundrel who, during the last recess, tried to flush one of the 2nd-grade boys down the toilet. WHAT! Sounds ridiculous! I never did such a thing, and later when I found out, who the boy was, not that I was seeking to know, I didn't even know him.

Until now, this is something I have never put into writing. It was not what you call a coveted award from Elementary School. But in and of itself was used by God as a lesson experience in life. The punishment for doing such a thing was probably right for the person who HAD DONE SUCH A THING IF SUCH A PERSON EXISTED. I had to stay in at recess until I wrote an apology stating I was sorry and would never do it again. Well, being the red-blooded American boy, I resolved that I would never apologize for something I had <u>not</u> done.

After several months of recess prison, I was doing fine until I heard the other elementary students on the playground as spring weather burst forth in all of its glory. I tell you, I couldn't take it any longer, and I weakened! I cracked under pressure and, within days, sold my soul to be released from the Elementary Recess Prison. Oh sure, criticize if you want, but it seemed like a life sentence for this red-blooded out-door farm boy. To this day, I have no idea what possessed this young man to pick me out of all those other boys for something that I knew nothing about. In fact, either someone tried to do this to him, and they never came forward to confess, or it was something concocted in the young man's mind.

Oh, I could understand if he had picked some "Recess Bullies" in the group. But no!! He picked me! HOW SPECIAL! I was not an angel, but it did seem a tad unfair to have this emotional trauma placed on me. I was too immature to sort it all out, but I was deeply hurt. I will never forget the embarrassment I endured as I struggled to find the right words to apologize. I wanted to shout out, "It wasn't me!! I'm innocent!! I didn't' do it!!" But the first and third-grade teachers had warned me that I would suffer the consequence if I didn't show a contrite heart. I questioned in my emotions if they even knew what contrite meant. Can you imagine if that would have happened today? They probably would have sent me to juvenile court; I may have spent time in the Big House. Who know?

I struggled in my loneliness, as there was no one to confide in and no one who would understand anyway. At least, that was how I felt. It was not something I could run home and tell my Mom and Dad or brothers about. Besides, I wanted to spare them the embarrassment. Even though Mom and Dad never said anything about it to me, I was sure they knew. It must have been God's understanding heart that caused them to be non-condemning, but it offered no place for comfort either. Today, I think their decision was right for me. But, at the time, as I cried on my pillow for several nights, I felt comfort from a Source[12]

---

[12] **John 14:16-19 NASB**

"I will ask the Father, and He will give you another Helper, (The Holy Spirit emphasis mine) that he may be with you forever; that is the Spirit of truth, whom the world cannot receive because it does not see Him or know Him, but you know Him because He abides with you and will be in you. I will not leave you as orphans; I will come to you. After a little while the world will no longer see Me, but you will see Me; because I live, you will live also."

I had never known before. And it was my first real encounter with a caring and loving God who came to me, a mere insufficient young man. There in the quietness of the night, I felt His love and comfort. Little did I know that in this and the next year, I would again need to know the Comforter's[12] heart and there crawl upon his lap and press my ear to His chest and press my fingers to his neck to sing, His Song?

During the next year, I had an appendectomy; I spent time in the hospital with what was thought to be Polio, where I was quarantined for a period of time and unable to see Mom and Dad. Finally, I fell very ill with virus-pneumonia. Mom said my two cheeks, left and right lower, looked like a pin-cushion from penicillin shots given every 3 hours. I was sick most of the year, and I'm not sure how many days I missed school. But thank goodness for the 5th/6th-grade teacher that gave her time to assist this broken student so I could pass to the next grade. I truly think that she saw the hurt that I endured and how it affected me mentally and physically. She got to know a kid where such behavior was not manifested in his everyday life. In part, it was her compassion and kindness that helped restore me to wellness and renew my respect for teachers, for which I am truly thankful. To this day, I can say that I am thankful for the boy in the 2nd- grade, that ignorantly, with false statements, brought me to the Comforter's arms, which gave me peace.

I believe it also made me a better father (Of course, you'll need to ask our four sons about that). I was very hesitant to discipline them unless I was absolutely convinced that they were at fault. But not to my surprise, there were many times when I knew for sure!

Now, young fathers, listen closely!

1) I had resolved to trust, rather than accuse, and offer unconditional acceptance and love as the norm rather than the exception.
2) In any case, to always be there with an understanding and a forgiving heart, balanced with discipline and love regardless of the situation.
3) I think they would say love continues to this day...

The incident of the 2nd-grade boy may be the reason why I have a good relationship with my adult sons today and may have been part of God's unseen plan.

Praise To The Lord by The Isaac
I Will Praise Him by The Isaacs
If That Is What It Takes by The Isaacs

Chapter 12

A GIFT OF HOPE
- THE TRANSPLANT

As you know, I am doing a word study, and I like the word "cured" better than the word "remission." It just seems to have a more lasting sound to it. But alas, remission remains the active word.

One time, when we were in the Doctor's office for a follow-up appointment, some flowers had just been delivered. Now, if you're like me, you have to know why or who would be sending flowers to the Doctor's office. The tag said, "Celebrating 15 years in remission." Actually, that might not have meant much to the average person, but I saw a smile come to Char's face as I read it to her, and then gentle tears. We didn't say much to each other right then, as we knew that our gift of a tender lasting love was indeed a "Gift from God." I'm not asking you to believe that, but if you want to know if it's true, you can ask those who have known us for many years.

We received hope from these words of encouragement, but the stark reality and emotions confirmed that this was a continuing journey in the unknown. When you think about it, the passage and continued life on this earth has always been out of our control. We faced it that day in real-time, as life is indeed fragile, and none of us knows how, when, or where this journey of life will take us. The expectation of having an eternal body with no pain, no sorrow, and no 2nd-grade boys, was appealing to me. But I doubt that any of us are fully prepared emotionally to take on such a body before our earth suit has deteriorated to the point of being beyond repair.

Interestingly, in the hospital, Char could always tell when she needed a transfusion. She would say to me, "It feels like life is leaving me." And I could see on her face the emotions she was experiencing at that moment. At about the same time, a nurse would bounce into the room and say, "Guess what, you are getting a transfusion today." I thought, wouldn't it be interesting if you could bounce into the lab downstairs and get a shot of courage, hope, forgiveness, compassion, a shot of…a shot of …

As Char had discovered when she became a follower of Christ, she would become a partaker of the divine nature and see the future more clearly through the lens of hope and peace.

THE DAY OF THE TRANSPLANT

On the day of the transplant, Char felt incredibly weak, as it had been a long, challenging, and sometimes what seemed like a cruel struggle to get to this point. It was scheduled for 10:00 am, then 11:00 am. The nurse came into the room about 12:00 pm stating, "Well, they're evidently having some problems, because I don't know where they are." Then the hours crept by with seemingly no movement on their part. Now, do you get the picture? The Chemo had killed Char's immune system, and the only way for her to have a chance at renewed life was the transplant. And in time, hopefully, it would build a new immune system. They were having trouble!! I was having trouble!!! As Char grew weaker, I knew that she was experiencing anxiety too.

A dear friend of ours from church, Debbie, had come to encourage Char as often as possible. What a great blessing she was to Char, and it also allowed me to go to our son's (Doug) house to clean up and take a short nap without interruptions. Debbie was there on the day of the transplant, too. We were truly thankful for her ministry, as our church was going through a change and the new pastor was either unable or unwilling to visit during the time of Char's hospitalization or time at home.

While waiting, Char asked me if I would sing a song that came to her mind. It is an old song that I had not sung for probably 35 years. I thought I could remember the words, in part. It was called "Whiter Than Snow."

> *"Whiter than snow, yes whiter than snow now wash me and I shall be whiter than snow. Lord Jesus I long to be PERFECTLY WHOLE. I want Thee forever to live in my soul. Break down every idol cast out every foe. Now wash me and I shall be whiter than snow. Whiter than snow, yes, whiter than snow, now wash me and I shall be whiter than snow."*

The words were taken in part from Psalms 51:7.

Char was waiting for a transplant that would give her a new immune system and hope for a renewed chance at life. There was also a day when she was forgiven and freely given a New Life, CHRIST'S LIFE.

COLOSSIANS 3:3,4 NASB

> *"For you have died and your life is hidden with Christ in God, when Christ who is our life, is revealed, then you also will be revealed with Him is glory."*

ROMANS 5:10 NASB

> *"For if while we were enemies we were reconciled to God through the death of His Son, much more, having been reconciled, we shall be saved by His life."*

Christ's life is eternal, and she became a partaker of his divine nature and was washed "Whiter Than Snow." She will one day receive an immortal body, free of disease, and perfectly whole physically. She said, "It was the only song she could think of." I think it was the only one because it was the right one for her at that moment. I can only hope I sang my part not too soft, not too loud, but just at the right time.

She received "The Transplant" (7/22/98), a date to remember because every doctor from that day forward will ask, "When did you receive your transplant? How long has your Leukemia been in remission?"

TWO DIFFERENT FAITHS

Char's Jewish Doctor was a handsome, intelligent, workaholic. During her stay in the hospital, there was a measure of bonding between this young man and her. When she first entered the hospital, he would come into the room, asking, "What do we have?" I think it was a reminder so that she did not remain in a state of denial. At first, it might have seemed not kind. But it was meant so she would live in the reality of the moment. I believe God does the same thing with us, "You have this problem, so don't remain in denial." Not all will believe they have a problem. But if we are honest with ourselves, we have all sinned.

I don't remember who started it, but they began citing Scriptures when he came into the room on his daily rounds. I'm not sure who enjoyed it the most, but this one thing I know, it was indeed a treat for me each day as they bantered back and forth what both believed to be God's Word. It was indeed Char's finest hour, as her memory quickened, and many verses she had previously read and studied returned with clarity giving credence to the Source of Power within her. Once in a while, the Dr. would come into the room, citing a verse in Hebrew. Char and I loved it, even if we couldn't understand a word. There was just something about his demeanor and enthusiasm that made it special! I believe he also received some joy during his long hours at the hospital when he entered her room. He knew we were in the Christian faith, and we knew his faith was Judaism. But it didn't matter, as the camaraderie was meaningful to both.

They had a lot more in common than one might imagine at first glance. He quoted a belief in the Old Testament as the Word of God, that it was worthwhile to memorize and share for comfort and support; that both believed in a Messiah, one believing He has already come, and one believing He has yet to come. Neither was intimidated by the quoting back and forth of Scripture in what both called the Bible. He made an interesting statement when he said that he liked the King James Bible, referring to the Old Testament. The New Testament was <u>not</u> particularly familiar to him because it is more about the New Covenant and a Forgiving Messiah.

The Doctor was not converted to Christianity, even though in the days ahead, the Bible states that many in Judaism will come to know Jesus as their Messiah. Nor was Char converted to Judaism. So, don't be too sad here, as he now knows a once little brunette gal with greying hair, now bald, that loves him and his Scripture as much as he does. For today, that may be all that was required.

Char finally received the transplant that offers new hope for a better tomorrow. Her appetite was a tad bigger than a sparrow, but she continued to gain strength. The initial recovery period was supposed to take about a year, but the first two years were the most critical that she remained in remission. After that, the chance for continued remission could increase for a short time. Let me assure you that this trial did not dampen our love or commitment to each other and has, if anything, served only to strengthen that resolve and commitment. Nor did it dampen our dedication and passion for the Lord Jesus Christ and His continuing plan.

It Matters to the Master by The Collingsworth Family
You're Still You by Josh Groban
You Raise Me Up By Selah

9/6/07

And he himself has promised us this: eternal life.

1 John 2:25 (TLB)

...here I am again, back in chemo for a leukemia they have yet to classify. Nine years leukemia-free. Thank You, Lord for those wonderful, precious years of life with Mel and our family, with our church family and friends. So many blessings! It scares me that this treatment may not work but the chance that it will work have the same odds. You have told me that You have set before me life and death, therefore choose life. I have chosen to do this chemo again. I believe You have given me more years, nevertheless, Your will be done... I know You have given me life on this earth but You have also given me Your Life. We tend to think of eternal life as a place rather than a Person. (Col 3:1-4) This day is not about my strength or courage (except what You give me), but its about my surrender to Your plan and purpose for me to bring glory to You.

9/10/04

The verse You have given me is
Ps. 71:17, 18

"Since my youth, O God, You have
taught me, and to this day I
declare Your marvelous deeds. Even
when I'm old and grey, do not
forsake me O God, till I declare
Your power to the next generation"

Jill Briscoe tells the story about
her friend who was a soccer coach
who told his players, who had just
tied a game, that if they find themselves in extra time to take risks
and go for the goal. Give it all
you've got and never give up! ☺

I seek your guidance
each day, Lord, sometimes
each hour. Give me ears to hear
and eyes to see You in everything. Give me, strength and
peace about his job and to see
You work that thru for him.
You, Lord Jesus, are our life & Life Coach

The eternal God is your refuge, and underneath are the everlasting arms.

Deuteronomy 33:27 (TLB)

Chapter 13

THE RETURN OF THE UNEXPECTED

A GIFT FROM GOD AND A LOVE SHARED

NINE AND A HALF YEARS HAD PASSED, REMARKABLY MUCH longer than the professionals expected. During her annual visit to the Doctor, he stated that she was his miracle girl. He noted that of the some of 263 in the experimental group, she was one of about 10 that they could identify as surviving that long. WOW! Let me tell you, she made use of it with her continuing study and mentoring of the women she so loved. Because of her weakened immune system, she stated that she had two speeds, this one, and stop.

It was then I coined the phrase, "I would rather burn out than rust out."

When we moved to the Antelope Valley, located just north of Metropolitan Los Angeles, we stopped at the overlook off Highway 14. It was there I asked her what she hoped to accomplish in the valley. She stated, "I want to teach the women of the valley 'How to Study the Bible.'" When Rev. Dan Jackson asked her to take on that task at First Baptist Church, she was more than ready after years of her own Bible study and 13 years with Bible Study Fellowship. I can tell you there were tears shed along the way, as even doing what God wants can sometimes be an emotional challenge. Char once stated that she had served with more pastors than anyone else on staff, as there seemed to be this ongoing turnover. But she loved it and loved serving the women.

One pastor stated, "Her love for God, His Word, and His people remains unmatched in my ministry experience."

In February, nine years after her remission, we had celebrated her best blood test since the transplant and remission. We were hopeful! It was not a wild party, but a dinner at Marie's! It was quiet because we both knew that the last nine years had been a "Gift from God" and a shared love.

In late April, her blood test revealed a drastic deterioration, and the race was on to find out the reason and what if anything could be done. It was not a complete surprise, as we had been traveling to a facility to have some blood withdrawn weekly or as required by the Doctor. It seemed there was an overabundance of iron in her blood, apparently caused by so many transfusions. But by withdrawing blood, the body would replace it with new blood.

Neither of us was looking forward to reliving the ordeal of her previous treatment and all of the seemingly near-death experiences she had endured. At least it seemed like that to me. But, we don't always have a choice about our experiences, just our destination.

With the new blood test and her immune system deteriorating, I asked the Doctor if I could take her to Hawaii to celebrate our 50th. He stated in no uncertain terms, "Be quick about it." So, we went to Hawaii with our youngest son Jon, and his family. It was a great time, and we celebrated it with hope and, quite frankly, with some risk as Char's immune system was in a very weakened condition. But as she wrote, "If you find yourself in extra time, take some risk and go for the goal."

Upon returning home, another blood test and bone marrow biopsy confirmed our fears; leukemia had indeed returned. The Doctor told her that she had six weeks to live if she did nothing. There were some options, and she chose the one that would give the best chance for the longest life. But, it carried the greatest risk of shortening her life too. Sometimes in life, there are no easy choices; indeed, this was one of those times. We were told the chances of survival were not good, but there was a chance. What do you do?

She asked the Doctor if he could keep her alive until the new expectant grandbaby was born. The Doctor hesitated, then stated, "They would try."

A child once prayed, "God why do you keep making new people, why don't you just keep the ones you have." The answer? He does, but differently. Would there be one girl gone and one girl sent? We didn't know for sure at that moment. Now Grandpa knows her as Lauren.

CHAR RETURNS TO UCLA

Women of the Word gather for prayer

Sue and Char

After her first remission, she was excited to return to the task set forth and the women she had loved and served for an extended time. The ministry continues to serve the valley's women and is a vital part of the church body in real-time. I am so grateful for the women leaders and volunteers that faithfully continue serving.

I was more than proud as Char realized her dream, and it was her destiny and time to shine.

On September 5, 2007, Char returned to UCLA Medical Center for Chemotherapy treatment. I remember the day well. Nothing was different from any other day, except the destination. She had some things to do around the house but promptly went to work at the church, where she served as the Director of Women's Ministry for 17 years.

As usual, I got ready for work, made the bed as my way of loving her, promising to meet her back home a little before noon. Upon her return, as we left home, she paused for a moment looking back into the house as if to sense she might not be returning. It was all I could do to keep from crying as the emotions of the moment surged through my body. I held her in my arms for a brief moment, and then off we went to Marie Callender's Restaurant for lunch, as we had done many times over the last 20 years. It was half price for us, as we were not big eaters and usually shared lunch. For the previous nine years, most days, having lunch together was a blessing! We saw some friends from church and visited a few moments before we embarked on the journey, not knowing if this would be our last time together at Marie's.

If you saw her that morning, you would not suspect her condition's seriousness when this continuing journey began. While she did not feel well most of the time, it didn't keep her down or from living a near as possible full life. As we went on this journey, it was much like the journey we experienced when it first began, quiet but together. When you have been married as long as we had, you don't always need to say something, as quietness can be serene, and there can be peace in being together. It was good to know that she was not facing this ordeal alone. Now, all of her strength and focus were ready for the battle at hand, and she was in the Master's care.

EPHESIAN 1:13 NASB

"In Him, you also, after listening to the message of truth, the gospel of your salvation – having also believed, you were sealed[10] in Him with the Holy Spirit of promise."

Neither one of us knew the outcome of the cancer treatment, but we knew her destination. It was that seemingly small decision made at about 14 years of age in becoming a follower of Christ that changed her life's path, sealing her final destination.

HIS UNSEEN PLAN IN ACTION

Char was now moving to her home going, in Heaven. In the last two days, she was in and out of sleep every 20 to 30 minutes, and I was exhausted. Late evening Jon came over so I could get some rest in the now deserted waiting room. About 3:00 am, he went home saying, "She wore us both out."

While sitting beside her hospital bed, a few hours before she fell into a deep sleep, I stood up and reached over to stroke her face with my hand, as I had many times over the years. <u>Only to hear her say, without ever opening her eyes, "I know who that is, because no one else, touches me like that."</u>

Later, when we were alone, I glanced out the hospital door window to observe a sea of white uniforms. The attending nurse said, For some time now, the doctors, nurses, technicians, and others had observed a man walking the hospital halls day and night. He gave evidence of his love for his wife, and they wanted to see this couple and pay their respects for a 50-year love union. One can only guess what was happening in that group, but I believe God's unseen plan was activated even during a dark hour for us.

In years past, I've had to ask for forgiveness from those who have lost a longtime love, for my lack of compassion and understanding thereof. I had no idea that I would, time and time again in the years to follow, need to crawl upon the lap of the "Babe of Christmas" and there renew my hope and passion for life, giving me the strength to sing His Song. It is a life with its present struggles, its joys for today, and its promises for tomorrow and eternity.

When I Cry by The Gaither Vocal Band
Angels Calling by The Tenors
Homeward by William Joseph – Within

Chapter 14

AT PEACE

INDEED, I WAS BLESSED MARRIED TO NOT A PERFECT LADY but a great lady.

Through rivers of tears, Char would love that her husband tells you her story of how a decision she made at 14 to follow Christ would change her, her life's path, and her final destination.

Char selected the following verses for our senior life's journey.

PSALMS 71:17,18 AMP

"O God, You have taught me from my youth, and I still declared your wondrous works and miraculous deeds. And even when I am old and gray-headed, O God, do not abandon me, Until I have declared Your mighty strength to this generation, Your power to all who are to come."

I CORINTHIANS 15:3-8 NASB

"For I delivered to you as of first importance what I also received, that Christ died for our sins according to the Scriptures, and that He was buried, and that He was raised on the third day according to the Scripture, and that

He appeared to Cephas, then to the twelve. After that He appeared <u>to more than five hundred brethren at one time</u>, most of whom remain until now, but some have fallen asleep; then He appeared to James, then to all the apostles; and last of all, as to one untimely born, He appeared to me also." (The apostle Paul)

The words above are an admonition, saying, "Check it out, as some of your brothers and sister are still alive," and it is this continued affirmation together with our own salvation experience in faith that lends credibility that our faith is true of Him! Our pastor clarified, stating, "You would never put the above statement, go ask your brothers and sisters as some are still alive" in a book, the Bible, if not true.

I hope that if you are not a follower of Christ, because of this writing, you will become one. And as you celebrate Christmas and Easter, as the birth and resurrection of Jesus, it is the continuation of an eternal love story of God loving His children. It is a story never forgotten that continues to this day. In that love story, He is standing beside you, saying, "Come unto to me all who are weary and heavy-laden, and I will give you rest." And there will be a time, without ever opening your eyes, you will know His touch, because no one else, no one else, touches you like that!

FINAL REST AND PEACE

She struggled to breathe, and I was cradling her in my arms, offering her a heart of love with encouragement, when her heart stopped. The nurse in the room sent out the signal, and medical professionals came running from all directions. As an extra, I was pushed off to the side and watched in amazement, and she was revived. I was asked to move into the hallway as they prepared her for relocation to Final Care. It's what extras are required to do. In the hallway, with a smile on her face, she was at last <u>at peace</u>. You could have reasonably thought that a miracle happened, and she was at last well again. I was hoping to ask her what she saw that gave her comfort, but it was not to be.

While she was in a deep sleep, I leaned over her bed and placed my face cheek to cheek with hers. She loved for me to do that, but this time something unique happened, as the alarms on the machines she was tethered to would go crazy. When I backed away, they would gradually stop. After several attempts with the same results, I asked the nurse if I was doing something wrong.

She said with somewhat of a quivering voice, "No, she knows you're here."

Can you believe that when God looks over the balcony of Heaven that He goes crazy thinking of how much He loves you, and you can know that He is there? Most of us cannot. Yet, it is true!

In those final moments, while we were alone, I opened her hand, and in the palm of her hand, as I had in young love years before, I took my index finger and wrote the letters I… L… U… I don't know for sure if she felt it, but I did, and the memories of our young love were rekindled.

That year marked the end of a journey of two earthly mortals, Char and I, who grew in love as crazy teens. It was the end of a never to be forgotten earthly love story, and she is now in the arms of her beloved Savior, the true love of her life, and she is at last well.

Do you want to know the truth here? I knew it would be difficult to continue, but I had no idea how difficult. After all, when you are crazy in love, should the final earthly parting be easy? I think not!

For me, I know He is there. I felt His touch as I have hundreds of times before, and without ever opening my eyes, I know Who it is because no one else, no one else, touches me like that.

In time, I, too, shall be well, in part because of His unseen plan and a 2nd-grade boy.

AT PEACE AND AT LAST WELL

GRIEF NEVER ENDS... BUT IT CHANGES.
IT'S A PASSAGE, NOT A PLACE TO STAY.
GRIEF IS NOT A SIGN OF WEAKNESS,
NOR LACK OF FAITH...
IT IS THE PRICE OF
LOVE

Author Unknown
I... L...Y... MEL

COLOSSIANS 3: 12-14 NASB

"So, as those who have been chosen of God, holy and beloved, put on a heart of compassion, kindness, humility, gentleness and patience; bearing with one another, and forgiving each other, whoever has a complaint against anyone; just as the Lord forgave you, so also should you. Beyond all these things put on love, which is the perfect bond of unity."

Peace by Bethel Music

The Story of My Life By Neil Diamond

Goodbye By Lionel Richie

I Believe by Diamond Rio

Knowing What I Know About Heaven by Guy Penrod

Revelation Song by Phillips, Craig & Dean

Reckless Love by Cory Asbury

Not Forgotten by Phil King & Cody Ray Lee

All People On Earth Do Dwell by The Martins

CPSIA information can be obtained
at www.ICGtesting.com
Printed in the USA
BVHW020537030221
599232BV00028B/1192